ANGER, RAGE, AND AGGRESSION

Funding to help underwrite the development of
the *15-Minute Focus* series has been generously provided by:

Maclellan

Maclellan Family Foundations

We partner with the courageous
to change the world.

The Sarah T. Butler Children's Center at the Pastoral Institute of Columbus, Georgia is dedicated to the mental health and well-being of children ages 1-18. This center provides comprehensive services that span psychological testing, intervention, therapy groups, and counseling. In all our activities we seek to inspire growth through faith, hope, and love.

Duplication and Copyright

P.O. Box 22185
Chattanooga, TN 37422-2185
423.899.5714 • 866.318.6294
fax: 423.899.4547 • www.ncyi.org

ISBN: 9781953945617
E-book ISBN: 9781953945624

Written by: Raychelle Cassada Lohmann, PhD
Published by National Center for Youth Issues
Starkey Printing • Chattanooga, TN, U.S.A. • March 2022

Contents

See page 89 for information about Downloadable Resources.

Introduction

"For every minute you remain angry, you give up sixty seconds of peace of mind."

~ Ralph Waldo Emerson

It is often said that the aftermath of a storm is worse than the storm itself, and the same is true about anger, rage, and aggression. Unfortunately, the repercussions of anger can be extensive, and the cleanup process is often met with hefty consequences and vast destruction. I know the cost of anger, rage, and aggression too well because I had difficulty regulating my own emotions as a child.

The hole in the back of my childhood bedroom door is a steadfast reminder of a child who didn't know how to weather the turmoil of her emotions. To this day, I can remember being so angry (about what, I do not recall), marching into my room, picking up a book, and hurling it at the back of my door. I can still hear the splintering sound of wood when the book made impact, leaving a hollow hole in the door and the feel of an immediate surge of remorse and fear of getting into trouble. A glance into my past makes me wish I could somehow go back and help that younger me cope with the intensity and destructive surge of emotions. Although I can't change my past, I can take my experiences and help others who work with angry youth, hence creating this very book.

I am intrigued by anger, rage, and aggression because I know how easy it is to become a prisoner of its intense power. I have devoted much of my career to helping angry, enraged, and aggressive youth, training educators, and assisting parents in better understanding their child's emotions. Did you know many of your students want nothing more than to free themselves from anger's powerful grip? Unregulated anger, impulsive and aggressive anger in nature, does not feel good to the carrier because they are the ones who are most often hurt by the emotion.

Did you know that anger-related issues are the most common reasons children are referred for mental health services?

Did you know that anger-related issues are the most common reasons children are referred for mental health services?[1] Prolonged periods of anger and aggression have been linked with depression, suicide, substance use, and more long-term psychological and physical health issues such as anxiety, cardiovascular disease, and premature death.[2/3] So, we have to help our students learn coping skills early. By doing so, we may be helping them live longer and more meaningful lives. I hope this book will help you better understand the scope of anger, rage, and aggression but, most importantly, support you in helping your students learn effective ways to manage anger, rage, and aggression.

Here are some suggestions to help you get the most out of this book:

1. Read the book under the assumption that all behavior serves a purpose. Meaning students act out for a reason. Our job is to uncover that reason to assist them in coping with their emotions and feelings.

2. Understand that perception is reality. What a student perceives to happen is their frame of reference and helps them justify their behaviors. If you want to help angry youth, you have to reach them from their perception of what occurred to provoke their anger.

3. Follow the chapters sequentially. The book follows a natural progression that unveils the multiple dimensions of anger.

4. Learn to identify the signs of anger, as well as the psychopathological symptoms that go well beyond anger, rage, and aggression.

5. Apply strategies to help youth learn to manage their anger.

If we commit to helping our students early, we can teach them valuable lessons that they can carry with them throughout life. In addition, there is a reward in knowing that the seeds we plant today may help ward off future heart attacks, high blood pressure, stroke, and relationship difficulties. As the proverb goes, "all the flowers of tomorrow are in the seeds of today."

Before we begin our deep dive into anger, rage, and aggression, I would like to share a story that touched my life and, more importantly, illustrates the importance of helping our students find peace from anger. At an event for one of my books, *The Anger Workbook for Teens*, an older adult male approached me and said, “You know I was one of those angry kids.” Looking up and making eye contact, I saw he wanted to spark a conversation and share his story, so I obliged. “You were?” I asked, noticing he had used past tense in his introduction. “What changed you?” He looked me in the eyes and said, “A triple bypass when I was forty and losing my wife to a divorce.” I wondered how many other hurts he had experienced from his anger. “Hmm, that’s a lot,” I replied. He paused and said, “It took that to make me realize that I had to change. You see, I found something...” He left me with the curiosity of wanting to know his secret to release anger. Inquisitively I asked him what he found. He smiled and looked me square in the eyes and confidently said, “I found inner peace.” [4]

I know firsthand that with your help, your students can learn to calm the angry storm within. They don’t have to live full of rage; they can remember to use assertion not aggression; and most importantly, they can find their *own* inner peace.

What Is Anger? Rage? Aggression?

Anybody can become angry—that is easy, but to be angry with the right person and to the right degree and at the right time and for the right purpose, and in the right way—that is not within everybody's power and is not easy.

-Aristotle

Odds are, when you think of anger, rage, and aggression you have an idea of what they entail, but how do you define them? Too often we couple anger, rage, and aggression into the same category. However, they have very distinct characteristics and vary in intensity, making them similar yet very different. In this chapter, we will explore the defining features of anger, rage, and aggression.

What Is Anger?

Anger is an emotion that most often surfaces when we aren't able to get our way, or we feel that someone has done something wrong. According to Dr. Paul Ekman, it is an emotion that falls into one of the seven basic universal emotions, along with joy, disgust, surprise, fear, contempt, and sadness.[5] Meaning that no matter where we are in the world, our facial expressions provide clear clues to how we are feeling, and others can interpret those feelings regardless of whether we speak the same language or not! Think about it. If we see someone who is seething mad, we may keep our distance because we don't want any part of their wrath. When you look at the seven emotions it's interesting that five are considered unpleasant.

The Seven Basic and Universal Emotions

Emotions create an impulse or urge to act. For example, when we are angry, we may have the urge to raise our voice, curse, or hit. If we are sad, we may resort to crying, sulking, or withdrawing. Emotions such as sadness, shame, guilt, and fear are often labeled as being unpleasant and uncomfortable because they leave us feeling vulnerable and out of control. Rather than feeling powerless and helpless, we may use anger to mask what we are really feeling. This emotional concealment is why anger is often referred to as a secondary emotion. Anger often becomes a first line of defense because it's an energy-producing emotion that creates a sense of being in charge. Plus it's easier to admit to being angry than feeling hurt, ashamed, or guilty.

As with other emotions, anger has some identifying characteristics that are important to understand. Research has noted anger undergoes a series of affective, cognitive, and behavioral processes. Each are explained in more detail.

- Like other emotions, anger has an **affective** factor, meaning it has a specific **feeling** attached to it. It feels different from other emotions such as happiness, which is on the opposite spectrum from anger. You know how it feels to be happy and elated about something. Now imagine feeling frustrated and angry. You probably felt the complete shift of thoughts. Anger and happiness are totally different feelings. One feels good and the other one not so much. This extreme dichotomy of feelings is why it's almost impossible to experience happiness and anger at the same time.

- After the anger makes its appearance, we begin to fuel our thoughts in justifying why we are mad. These thoughts are referred to as the **cognitive** process of anger. Angry thoughts have a purpose to prepare us to act. When we are angry our thoughts help us make plans to make a wrong right. Our thoughts don't cause a problem because thoughts are powerless unless we buy in to them.
- Again, our thoughts aren't a problem unless we act on them. Rather, it's our actions that can lead to big consequences, and that leads us to the **behavioral** process of anger. [6]

Try This!

Anger varies in intensity. For example, most of us don't go from 0 to 10 instantaneously, but instead, we go through a series of escalations. That series can be described in words, and the vocabulary we use can show how angry we are. For example, words like *agitated*, *frustrated*, *irritated*, *irate*, and *hostile* are words that vary in intensity. You can use a technique known as scaling to help assess their experience in terms of steps. Let's give scaling a try with anger and words.

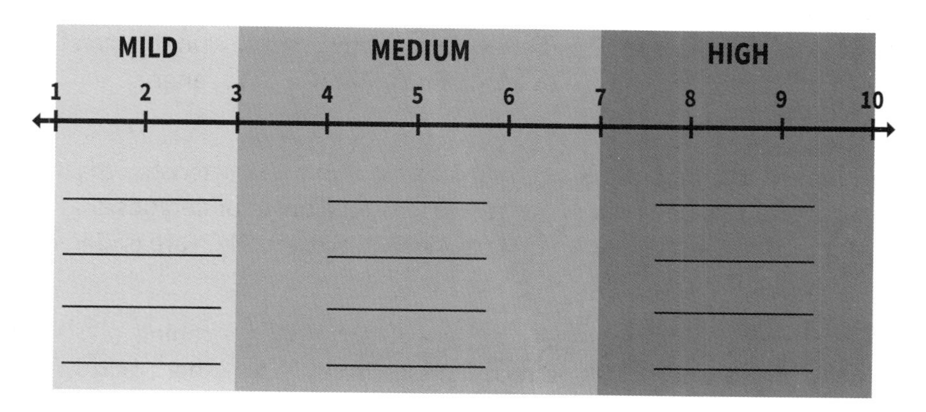

On the anger intensity scale, write the words you use to describe your anger. Level one on the scale is a word that you use when becoming angry, and level ten is when you are at your angriest. For example, some of the words that I use include *annoyed*, *irritated*, *mad*, or *ticked off*. Scaling is a great way to help students express the feelings they have when their anger is escalating. Recognizing the early signs of escalation can help them step outside themselves and put in words how they feel. It also helps build self-awareness and links thoughts to feelings and behaviors.

What Is Rage?

Rage is a form of intense anger...

Rage is a form of intense anger, and it can be either productive or problematic, depending on how it's handled. If we think about anger in terms of intensity, rage would be at the top of our scale. People who are filled with rage often struggle with self-awareness and emotional regulation. They lack communication skills and struggle to express their thoughts and feelings. Does this description bring any students to mind?

Students who experience chronic anger and rage are at risk for health problems. For example, intense levels of anger and rage have been associated with heart disease, high blood pressure, and even premature death—a few of the many reasons to help students with emotional regulation.

On the flip side, rage can be proactive when used constructively and create needed change. For example, cultural rage has been described to combat social injustice, inequality, and systemic oppression. Both anger and rage can be used to prepare us to fight the good fight.

What Is Aggression?

Aggression is an intent to harm. It often occurs with anger, but it doesn't have to. You can be aggressive and not angry, and you can be angry and not aggressive. Aggression provides us with a sense of power and can fuel our anger. Aggression coupled with rage can be catastrophic. When paired together, you may see a student hitting another student, throwing a chair across the room, cursing out a teacher, shouting obscenities in the hallway, or even breaking things. Students who have difficulty regulating intense emotions like anger can be challenging to manage. For example, consider the case of Dylan.

A Student's Story

Dylan, a sophomore, was escorted into my office by the principal. Unsure of what was happening, I quickly assessed the situation. Dylan's fists were clenched at his side, he was breathing heavily, and sweat was dripping from his brow. The principal, in a stern tone, commanded Dylan to "Have a seat, and I'll get with you once I get a statement from the other student." The air seemed to be sucked right out of my office at that moment. I recognized my senses were on alert. Looking into Dylan's eyes, I thought, "This student is going to explode!"

You see, Dylan had just been pulled off another student in a fight, and I was fortunate to be his next stop before making his way into the principal's office. I had heard that it took multiple people to peel him off the student, so I knew he was off the Richter scale of anger. Quickly assessing Dylan's behaviors, I decided to help him do something he didn't know how to do for himself: *calm down*.

I knew that Dylan was in no mood to talk. Reliving or contemplating what had just happened would only escalate his anger, taking him in the opposite direction of where I needed him to be. I decided to change the environment. I got up from my desk, dimmed the lights, turned on some soft background music, and told him to just hang with me for a few minutes and catch his breath. I will never forget the look on his face. He looked confused because, wasn't I supposed to ask him about what happened? Isn't that what we all do when there's an altercation? *Not this time, Dylan*.

I continued working on my computer, gently tapping the keyboard. Eventually, Dylan either got bored or calmed down enough to talk. Regardless of the reason, the cool-down tactic had worked, unbeknownst to Dylan. He looked at me and said, "He just made me so mad that I blacked out. I don't remember anything." It was his vocabulary "blacked out" that let me know Dylan's anger had escalated to the dangerous point of rage. Language does matter. I wondered how often had he "blacked out" in his life?

1. Can you identify the differences between anger, rage, and aggression?

2. Describe the feeling (affective), thought (cognitive), and action (behavioral) processes that occur in anger?

3. How can anger and rage be productive in creating change?

- Rage is an intense form of anger.

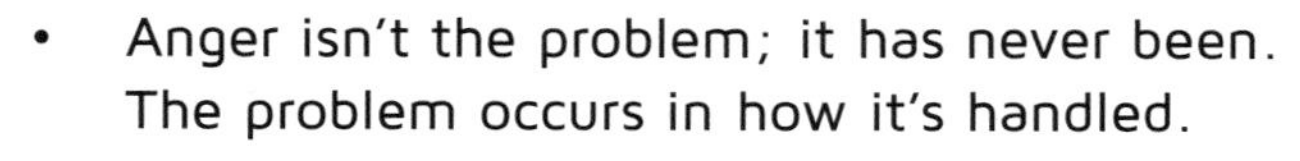

- Anger isn't the problem; it has never been. The problem occurs in how it's handled.
- Problems are the result of our actions.

- Aggression is the intent to harm another person or thing.

2 Beyond Anger, Rage, and Aggression

Mental health "is a state of well-being in which an individual realizes their abilities, can cope with the normal stresses of life, can work productively, and can make a contribution to their community. In this positive sense, mental health is the foundation for individual well-being and the effective functioning of a community."[7]

– World Health Organization (WHO)

Over thirty-two mental disorders, such as major depression and intermittent explosive disorder (IED), include anger, aggression, or irritability as a symptom.[8] Nearly half of all mental health issues begin by age fourteen, and most cases are undetected and untreated.[9] As a professional in the educational setting, you know firsthand how emotional and mental well-being can impact your students' ability to function socially and academically. As such, you must recognize how anger, rage, and aggression can manifest within other mental health conditions. In this chapter, we'll explore some of the most common youth mental health concerns, and we'll examine anger's part within each of these conditions.

Anxiety

What It Is

Anxiety is a typical childhood and mental health illness. People with anxiety frequently have intense, excessive, and persistent worry and fear about everyday situations. Unlike stress, anxiety persists even after a perceived threat has passed. Anxiety disorders are classified in various ways: generalized anxiety, panic disorder, phobias, social anxiety, and separation anxiety. It is estimated that about 7 percent of youth ages 3 to 17 years have been diagnosed with an anxiety disorder.[10]

Researchers have shown that being prone to anxiety is associated with episodes of anger.[11] Understanding this relationship can help you design interventions addressing anxiety coping skills, which can decrease anger. Both anger and anxiety cause an increased alert sense and activate the fight-or-flight stress response. Fight or flight is a neurobiological response that is triggered when we feel threatened and in danger. When we feel we are in danger, our bodies release surging energy hormones, such as cortisol and adrenaline, into the blood system, resulting in a keen sense of awareness and strength. For safety, we are preparing to fight or flee the situation. When we are anxious or angry, our bodies react similarly, so when working with a student with chronic anger, ask yourself, “Is anxiety fueling the anger?” If so, you need to help the student work through stress and anxiety, because if you just focus on the product of the anxiety—the anger—you’re only putting a Band-Aid on the problem, and it will keep occurring until the underlying issue is addressed.

What It May Look Like in School

Children with anxiety may procrastinate or avoid situations that cause stress and discomfort. For example, think about a child who fears math. As a means of avoidance, this student could have chronic school absenteeism; may hide in the restroom or seek solace in the counselor’s office during math class; or, worse yet, get physically sick before each class. If forced to be in anxiety-producing situations, the student may even lash out in anger as a diversionary tactic to avoid math. The anxiety causes so much distress that the student perceives they are in danger and will do whatever it takes to keep from facing what they fear most.

How It's Treated

Anxiety is treatable. Medications in conjunction with cognitive-behavioral therapy (CBT) are highly effective in treating anxiety.[12] Although CBT focuses on changing how students think about and interact with their fears, it also emphasizes stress-reduction techniques through relaxation skills such as deep abdominal breathing, progressive muscle relaxation (PMR; slowly tensing areas of your body starting at your feet and working your way to your head and then slowly releasing in reverse order until all of the tension has drained out through your feet), and healthy self-talk (i.e., thinking helpful words, praising affirmations, or self-assuring statements).

Attention Deficit Hyperactive Disorder

What It Is

Working in a school setting, you are no stranger to Attention Deficit Hyperactive Disorder (ADHD). ADHD is one of the most common neurodevelopmental disorders affecting children. It is estimated that 9 percent of children have been diagnosed with the disorder, with boys receiving the diagnosis more than girls.[13] ADHD presents as three types: inattentive, hyperactive-impulsive, and combined.[14] The inattentive type is marked by distraction, lack of task completion, and losing items. The hyperactive-impulsive type involves fidgeting, impulsivity, difficulty sitting still, talking too much, and interrupting others. Lastly, the combined type is the most common, including inattentive and hyperactive-impulsive characteristics.

What It May Look Like in School

Children with ADHD have difficulty regulating their emotions. Like anxiety, ADHD and anger are usually found together. Why? Because of ADHD, students often struggle with self-control, and when they feel something, like anger, it's not uncommon for them to act on how they feel without thinking through the consequences of their actions. For example, students with ADHD may struggle with paying attention, but they may also be quick to throw a tantrum or strike out toward others due to poor impulse control skills. In addition, they may refuse to follow instructions, especially if they are asked to stop doing something they enjoy doing.

Think of the student who is immensely engaged and enjoying a classroom task, and then the teacher moves on to another activity. This student may have difficulty transitioning between jobs and not want to stop what they're doing. So one minute, things are going well because the child is attentively engaged in the activity. However, the next minute, the child throws a fit and is escorted out of the room by the administration because they had difficulty transitioning between tasks. Students with ADHD may also struggle with peer relationships and get aggressive if things don't go their way. However, unlike some other mental disorders, kids with ADHD don't have ill intent when they act out. Instead, they do it impulsively, without thinking through the consequences of their behaviors.

How It's Treated

Students with ADHD can be taught to recognize how they feel and communicate and express themselves appropriately. These youth benefit from learning how to calm down and think through situations. They tend to respond well to behavioral therapy to learn self-regulation skills. These youth thrive in environments that are consistent and provide concise instruction. They don't do well with ambiguity. Children with ADHD also do well with behavioral systems and charts with built-in rewards because there are clear expectations for their behaviors. They reap the benefits of following through with appropriate actions. However, they also see the consequences if they don't abide by the contract.

One thing to note about behavioral reinforcement systems with ADHD youth is that it needs to be short-term. For example, asking them to perform a specific behavior for a week before getting the reinforcement may be too much for a hyperactive-impulsive kid. Rather, begin small, like accomplishing the task in a daily class period. Once these students demonstrate the skills outlined in the plan, you can increase the time frame. Besides the school system, medications and parent training have also proven beneficial in treating ADHD.

Depression

What It Is

More than a case of the blues, depression is a severe mood disorder characterized by feeling sad, irritable, and hopeless. Symptoms can go on for weeks, months, and even years. It is estimated that depression affects about 13 percent of the nation's youth ages 12 to 17. [15] Chronic depression has been associated with suicide, one of the leading causes of death in children and young adults ages 10 to 24.[16]

Depression in childhood and adolescence can manifest somewhat differently than in adults. For example, moodiness and anger are more common signs of depression in children and teens than sadness. A common mistake is thinking that depressive symptoms are typical youth behavior. Depression is a severe mental health illness and is often comorbid with anxiety. As an educator, you must recognize the signs of depression and seek assistance if you believe one of your students shows depressive symptoms.

What It May Look Like in School

A student with depression may have difficulty in school academically and socially. They may not be taking care of themselves in terms of good hygiene, eating healthily, or getting too much or not enough sleep. These students have difficulty concentrating, lack empathy, and do not care about anything or anyone, including themselves. They may have low self-worth and be numb to their emotions. Students with depression are notorious for pushing people away, and they may use anger as a pivotal force to do so. As a result, they may be defiant and verbally aggressive. However, this may also be a rouse for keeping people away. These factors may contribute to increased irritability, making these youth more prone to angry outbursts. As an educator, the best thing you can do for these kids is to remain present. Do not let them nudge you out of their lives. Let them know that no matter how hard they push, you are there to support them.

How It's Treated

Like anxiety, depression is treatable with therapy and medication. Making sure the basic needs, such as nutrition, exercise, and sleep, are met is one of the first lines of defense with depression. As for treatment modalities, CBT has been referred to as the gold standard for treating many mental disorders, and depression is no different. For depression, the therapeutic focus is on working with unhelpful thoughts and helping students reframe or change their troublesome thoughts into healthier ones. Rather than bottling up their feelings, youth with depression also need to learn to express themselves and communicate how they feel. Also, having something to look forward to is an integral part of the treatment process. A way to get them moving in a forward motion is to set attainable goals.

Aside from CBT, other therapies, such as dialectical behavior therapy (DBT), are also effective in treating depression. DBT is a means of helping youth manage their painful emotions by grounding them in the present and teaching them mindfulness and relaxation. For younger children, art therapy, which uses expression through visual art, is helpful, as is play therapy, which uses toys to help children express and model appropriate behaviors.

Disruptive, Impulse-Control, and Conduct Disorders

In this section, we will explore a group of disorders that can cause our students to become angry, act out aggressively, and possibly throw a fit of rage. These disorders are known as Disruptive, Impulse-Control, and Conduct Disorders, and they can seriously impact a student's everyday life. In this section, we'll focus on the three that are most connected to anger, rage, and aggression. These conditions are Conduct Disorder, Intermittent Explosive Disorder, and Oppositional Defiant Disorder.

Conduct Disorder

What It Is

Conduct Disorder (CD) is typically diagnosed in childhood. It is characterized by a callous disregard for aggression toward others, bullying, hitting, cruelty, and violence.[17] The behavior of these youth is often described as hostile. Unlike other disorders that seem to be directed internally, conduct disorders are externally driven and affect others. Children exposed to verbal or physical abuse or who have been sexually traumatized are at a higher likelihood of having CD. Also, youth who have a parent who uses substances regularly are at an increased risk of having the disorder.

What It May Look Like in School

Children with CD frequently destroy property and are physically violent toward animals and people. They have a hard time following rules and are often defiant toward authority figures. These students may be manipulative, lie, push, hit, bite, bully, intentionally hurt other living things, steal, and vandalize property. A significant characteristic of this disorder is these youth tend to show no remorse. Their response is actually the opposite; their destructive tirades often bring about a sense of satisfaction and gratification. Due to their extreme behaviors, these students often have been involved with the juvenile justice system. Early intervention is key to helping these youth, because CD usually develops into antisocial personality disorder in adulthood. So, the earlier the intervention, the better the outcome.

Intermittent Explosive Disorder

What It Is

Intermittent Explosive Disorder is an impulse-control disorder that typically begins in teens but can be present in children as young as six; however, it is not diagnosed younger than age six.[18] It is estimated that 2.7 percent of children and adults in the US are affected by IED, and males are affected by it at a higher rate than females. IED is commonly associated with other mental health conditions such as anxiety, depression, and substance use. [19] Due to the explosiveness and impulsiveness of IED, these youth are also at a higher risk of self-harm and suicide.

What It May Look Like in School

Children with IED have difficulty controlling their anger and often have aggressive and impulsive outbursts with no provocation or triggering event. The behavior is grossly out of proportion to the situation. IED can manifest through verbal and physical aggression, and episodes may last up to thirty minutes. Some common signs of IED include being argumentative, getting into fights, threatening and assaulting others, throwing objects, and damaging property. During an episode, youth are usually unable to restrain themselves, so it's best if they are in a safe environment to release their emotions. Youth often describe an IED episode as being out of control in their behavior. Remember, a vital characteristic of these kids' behavior is extreme anger that is out of proportion to the situation. Even the slightest trigger can set them off. After an episode, youth are often remorseful and apologetic because they know the severity of their anger.

Oppositional Defiant Disorder

What It Is

Oppositional defiant disorder (ODD) is characterized by a frequent and persistent pattern of angry/irritable mood, argumentative/

defiant behavior, or vindictiveness that may significantly impair social functioning.ODD is often referred to as a milder version of CD, and it is diagnosed at an earlier age. Symptoms of ODD include anger and irritability, defiance, and being argumentative and spiteful. For children younger than five years, to be diagnosed, the problematic behavior must occur on most days for at least six months. For children five years and older, the behavior must occur at least once per week for six months. [20]

What It May Look Like in School

Children with ODD are often argumentative, uncooperative, and disobedient. They may have frequent temper tantrums, defy authority figures, and intentionally do things to annoy or anger others. Do you know the saying "misery loves company"? These students struggle behaviorally, so having someone else feel the same thing is fair game. These youth may seek revenge or retribution if they feel they have been wronged. They will often question the rules and find ways to break them or, better yet, find a loophole in the rules and work around them. They frequently deflect responsibility and justify their problematic behaviors. Although you may be thinking, *I know a lot of students who fall into this category*, remember with mental illness, these issues are at an extreme level and significantly affect the student's ability to function.

How They Are Treated

Cognitive-behavioral therapy (CBT) is a highly efficacious treatment for Disruptive, Impulse-Control, and Conduct Disorders. Using this approach, youth learn to identify situations that trigger them emotionally and understand how their thoughts and feelings can provoke anger and aggression. CBT is a problem-solving approach that helps students work through complex problems and weigh out the consequences of their behaviors before acting. Students also learn how to relax their bodies and calm their minds to alter their thinking and, in turn, change their behaviors. Family therapy, specifically parent management training that focuses on responding to challenging behaviors, is also highly effective in helping these youth.

If you have a student struggling with one of these disorders, the most important thing you can do is build rapport. These youth often have a lot of mistrust; they need to know who they can turn to in times of need. Be cautioned that building rapport is often not easy with these youth. They may not trust authority and will push away or even lash out if someone tries to quickly get close to them. Sadly, many of these students don't respect themselves, so it isn't easy for them to respect others. A good rule of thumb when working with these youth is to separate the behavior from the student. It's okay to be disappointed in the behavior, but not the child. Each day needs to be a new day for these students. These students stay in trouble more often than not, and their problematic behavior trumps all the other things they do well.

Look At This!

This chapter has explored some typical childhood mental disorders and how anger, aggression, and rage can be a symptom of their condition. The following chart captures the overlap between the two.

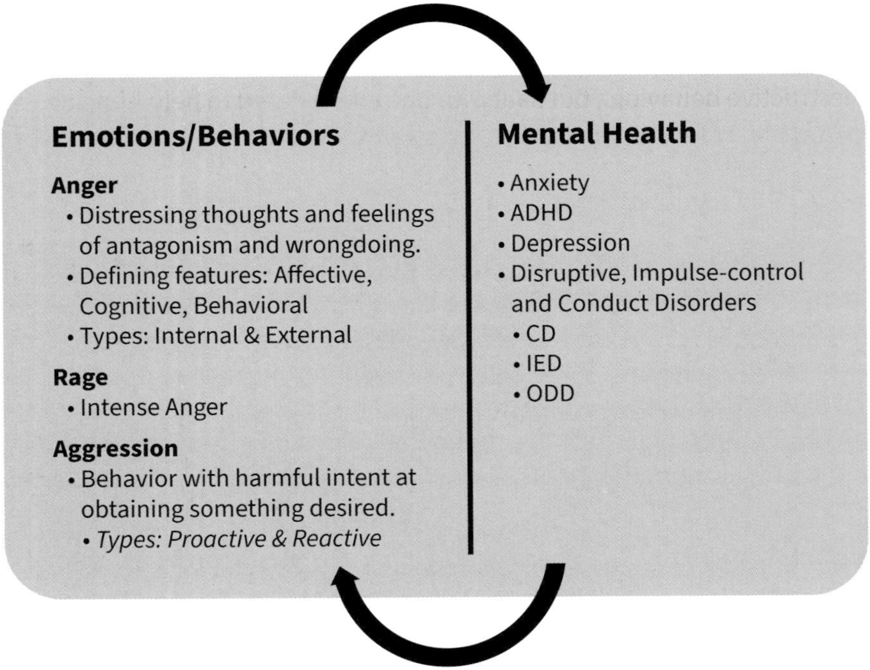

Emotions/Behaviors

Anger
- Distressing thoughts and feelings of antagonism and wrongdoing.
- Defining features: Affective, Cognitive, Behavioral
- Types: Internal & External

Rage
- Intense Anger

Aggression
- Behavior with harmful intent at obtaining something desired.
  - *Types: Proactive & Reactive*

Mental Health
- Anxiety
- ADHD
- Depression
- Disruptive, Impulse-control and Conduct Disorders
  - CD
  - IED
  - ODD

A Student's Story

Ian got home from school and went straight to his room. He slammed the door so hard the windows rattled, and he threw his backpack across the room. He couldn't get a hold of himself, and he knew it. He unleashed by slamming his fist in the wall so hard that the skin peeled back from his knuckles. Ian didn't feel the pain though; all he felt was a burning rage. He reached down and swiped his arm across the top of the dresser, sending everything flying across the room as though it were caught up in hurricane-force winds. After a few minutes of physically unleashing, Ian began to feel a little calmer. He looked at the aftermath of his vengeance and buried his face in his hands. He was breathing heavily and shaking uncontrollably. As he continued to regain composure, he assessed the damage and sighed. Looking around his room, he saw yet another volatile episode. His room looked like a war zone, and it was all his doing. Ian knew his anger was out of control, and he didn't know what was wrong with him. And worse, he didn't know how to stop the raging fire. During his anger, the only thing that made him feel better was destruction, but on the flip side, afterward, he felt horrible. Ian's tantrums had caused pain to himself, friends, and family. He was afraid that one day he might hurt someone he loved. Unfortunately, Ian was constantly punished for his short fuse and destructive behaviors, but sadly, no one ever offered to help him. Ian, like so many other students, suffered from IED.

QUESTIONS to CONSIDER

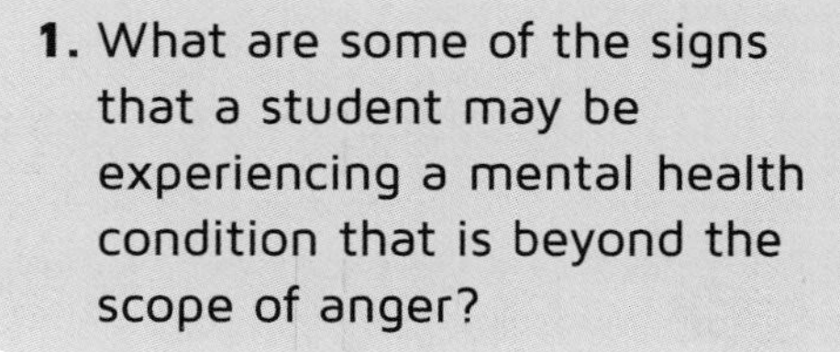

1. What are some of the signs that a student may be experiencing a mental health condition that is beyond the scope of anger?

2. What are some common mental health concerns present in the population of students that you work with?

3. Now that you better understand how anger manifests in mental health conditions, what role will you play in helping your students?

- Behavioral therapies focused on thoughts, feelings, and behaviors are evidence-based treatment approaches to helping youth with mental health issues.
- When working with angry youth, it's essential to recognize and support students struggling with mental health challenges.
- Although many of our students may have some of the symptoms present in the disorders discussed in the chapter, it's important to note that with mental health issues, these symptoms are more extreme, severe, and span beyond what is considered typical child or adolescent behavior.

3 What Causes Anger, Rage, and Aggression?

How much more grievous are the consequences of anger than the causes of it.

~Marcus Aurelius

What causes anger? I wish I had an answer to that loaded question, but in truth, many factors, known as triggers, contribute to getting angry. Triggers are situations or circumstances that ignite a spark within us. Knowing what causes these sparks is an essential step in anger management. In this chapter, we will explore common reasons students get angry and what triggers their anger.

Common Reasons for Anger

Students don't get angry without a reason; there is more to anger than meets the eye. If we want to help our students, we must go below the surface of what's happening to unveil the true culprit behind their anger. The following are some common reasons students report getting angry.

1. They feel misunderstood.
2. They feel unheard.
3. They feel embarrassed.
4. They feel the situation is unfair.
5. They feel singled out.
6. They feel hurt.

7. They feel anxious or stressed.
8. They are hungry or tired.
9. They are unable to communicate or express their thoughts and feelings.

Identifying Triggers

Have you ever felt like you're walking through a minefield with some of your students, avoiding saying or doing anything that may set them off? In these situations, it's essential to identify what's causing the problem. But, again, it's important to note that it's not the trigger causing the problem but rather how the student reacts to the problematic trigger.

Behavior is a form of communication. When working with an angry student, remember that all behavior serves a purpose, and perception is reality. Next, try to step back and ask what they are trying to communicate through their anger that they can't express in other ways.

Situational Triggers

Just like there are common causes of anger, there are also common triggers. The following are some triggering events.

Students:

1. being told "no" or that they can't do something
2. being told upsetting news
3. being left out of situations or events, especially ones that involve peers
4. being ignored and feeling unimportant
5. being picked on, insulted, called names, and singled out
6. being lied to
7. being accused of something they didn't do
8. being interrupted
9. being behind and lost or losing an event

Environmental Triggers

Life events can also trigger anger. Some everyday events may include the following:

1. Traumatic events, like a car accident
2. Parental conflict or divorce
3. Death of a loved one
4. Adoption issues—you may see this come out in adolescence as they begin to explore their identity, and abandonment issues arise
5. Exposure to natural events, like a hurricane
6. Change of residence
7. Loss of caregiver's job
8. Abuse, in any form
9. Physical illness
10. Switching schools

Think About This

Sadly, like millions of other children in the US, Jordan lives in poverty. She goes home hungry to a bare refrigerator. She often feels as though the world is working against her. She thinks no one understands and all the other kids at school don't have it as bad as she does. These thoughts make her angry. She rarely sees her mom because she works two jobs to make ends meet. Jordan also must take care of her two younger siblings, and on top of housework and prepping dinner, she does her best to complete her homework. Jordan frequently falls asleep in class, and when called out, she becomes very argumentative. She doesn't have many friends because she doesn't have time to socialize. She also doesn't have any electronic devices, so she feels like an outcast.

As an educator, you probably know kids like Jordan. Think of all the events and situations that may be triggering Jordan's anger. Is it any surprise that she comes to school with a chip on her shoulder? All too often, it's Jordan's anger and argumentative personality that gets front-and-center attention. However, if we'd take the time to hear her perception of what's occurring, we may very well understand her behavior.

A Student's Story

Madi was highly irritable. She had a terrible week, and things weren't getting better. Everyone was always telling her to look on the bright side, but when your parents are getting a divorce, your grades are falling, and you break your arm right before soccer tryouts, there's no light at the end of the tunnel.

Soccer was Madi's way of coping with stress, a place where she could pound out her feelings on the field. Without an outlet, Madi felt trapped in her life, and it was taking a toll on her. She wasn't eating, sleeping, or exercising. The more Madi thought about her situation, the angrier she became. The thought *It's not fair!* was on a constant loop in her mind. She felt her identity was being stripped away from her. So, when Mr. James called her out in math class for sleeping, she became embarrassed, which made her mad. He wouldn't stop riding her case. She'd had enough! Madi pushed her chair back with so much force that her desk flipped onto the floor, making a loud bang. The other students gasped, awaiting what would happen next. Madi stared Mr. James square in the eyes and told him what he could do with himself in not so many nice words.

In this case, you can see how many factors contributed to the cause of Madi's anger, rage, and aggression. Mr. James wasn't the sole cause of Madi's anger, but his comments were triggering. Too often, we look for a single reason to understand our students' behaviors, but it isn't that easy. In working with Madi, you'd want to help her cope with what's going on at home, help her deal with the broken arm, and take better care of herself. In doing so, you'll help Madi with her anger, rage, *and* aggression.

1. Beyond those listed, what are some other reasons students get angry?

2. In your experience, what are some other situational events that trigger anger?

3. Can you think of any other environmental situations that can trigger anger besides those mentioned?

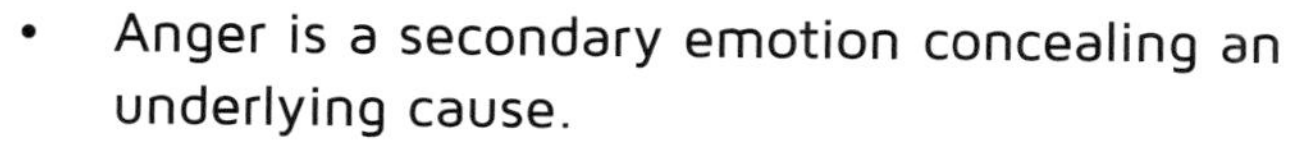

- Anger is a secondary emotion concealing an underlying cause.
- Psychosocial stressors are intense situations that affect our students' ability to function socially, emotionally, and academically.
- All behavior serves a purpose.
- Perception is reality.
- As educators, we must see the big picture of what's going on in our students' lives.

4 Ways People Handle Anger and Aggression

It is wise to direct your anger towards problems— not people; to focus your energies on answers—not excuses.

– William Arthur Ward

There are many ways people express their anger. Some may lash out verbally, and others may hold it in. I was reminded of the latter at a conference I presented at once. After the presentation, an attendee approached me and shared, "I have always had anger management problems, but no one ever believed me because they thought I was quiet and shy." She explained that her easygoing personality was a detriment because her anger stayed pent up on the inside. Her only way to deal with anger was to beat herself up through self-harm. Her arms bore the scars of her pent-up anger. In this chapter, we will explore the different ways students may express anger and aggression, so we can recognize that even our quiet students can have anger issues.

What Are the Types of Anger?

Rage is anger in an extreme form, so for the sake of this chapter, rage will be addressed in our conversations about anger. People express anger internally and externally.

External Anger

External anger is probably the most common type of anger. It's the type that we think about when we picture someone being mad. We often see this type of anger displayed in movies and TV shows. Take, for example, the ever-popular Bruce Banner, who gets triggered by an external event and immediately begins to transform. Ultimately the toll of anger leads Banner to turn into the Incredible Hulk. Although fictional, the Hulk does figuratively show the cost anger can have on us from a reasoning and physical stance. Although our students don't rip out of their clothes and turn green, outward anger does lead to uncanny transformations. Angry students are often more powerful when they are angry than calm, and they can be difficult to reason with as well.

In school, external anger may display as:

- **being judgmental:** These students may be susceptible to jealousy and resentment.
- **being overwhelmed:** These students feel that there's too much to deal with, making them more irritable and prone to anger.
- **being retaliatory:** These youth may feel as though they have been done wrong, and it's up to them to make sure justice prevails.

In school, outward anger may look like this:

- Breaking things
- Cursing
- Hitting
- Shouting
- Throwing things

Internal Anger

Internal anger, also referred to as self-inflicted anger, is directed inwardly and co-occurs with low self-esteem and guilt. Unless your student tells you they struggle with anger, you may have no idea because they seem to have it all together on the outside. Take, for example, the conference attendee who held in her anger to the point of self-harm. Her arms will forever serve as a reminder of her uncontrollable anger. Internal anger is usually self-directed; it isn't about other people or things but themselves. Listen to what your students say. Their word choice holds the key to determining if they struggle with suppressed anger.

In school, inward anger may look like this:

- Self-harming behaviors include binge/purging food, burning, or cutting into the skin.
- Unhealthy self-talk, such as:
  - I'm stupid.
  - No one likes me.
  - I always screw things up.
- Writings or drawings that illustrate a distorted self-image or self-harm. These drawings may be dark, showing disfigured images, weaponry, or blood.
- Restricting oneself from enjoyable activities or controlling food by not eating enough or overeating.

What Are the Types of Aggression?

Remember the distinction between anger and aggression: anger is an emotion, and aggression is a behavior. They two may or may not co-occur together. There are two predominant types of aggression in the literature: proactive and reactive.[21]

Proactive Aggression

Students who use **proactive aggression**[22] are often unprovoked and after something. These students will strategically calculate ways to get what they want. We would often perceive these students as manipulative as they appear calm and in control. This is the student who will wait to teach the person they are mad at a lesson for doing them wrong. Unfortunately, these youth often lack empathy and have difficulty relating to how their actions may affect others. These students often tell themselves that the person has it coming to them or their punishment is well-deserved. It's easy to take their lack of remorse or empathy as not caring, but don't let their actions fool you. These youth struggle to relate with others, and they often don't know how to communicate or express their feelings.

In school, proactive aggression may look like this:

- Encouraging other students to gang up on another student.
- Hitting a peer to gain respect from a group.
- Bullying another student (bullying is a form of proactive aggression).

Reactive Aggression

Reactive aggression is the defensive, revengeful response to a perceived threat, and it's closely linked with external anger. Students with this type of aggression may be impulsive, volatile, and overreact to minor provocations.[23]

In school, reactive aggression may look like this:

- Punching a peer because they called them a name.
- Yelling at the teacher for accusing them of something they didn't do.
- Throwing a backpack down the hall when someone steps on the heel of their new shoe.

Try This!

I have found that teaching students to talk themselves down from their anger can be a beneficial tool. Too often, students who struggle with anger get worked up over the small stuff, leading to enormous consequences. Teach them to recognize when they get triggered by working through the following questions:

1. Is this situation worth my time and energy?
2. Is it worth ruining my day?
3. Is it worth the consequences?
4. What do I have to gain by acting out? What might I have to lose?

I have my clients write down their answers on a small card and take a screenshot of them to refer to the next time they're in an anger-provoking situation. I do this because impulsive clients need constant and accessible reminders that they control their behavior. Plus, if the questions and answers are readily available, they are more apt to use them.

A Student's Story

Lucas wanted the toy robot Elijah was playing with, so he walked over and took it from him. Elijah watched as Lucas walked off with his toy. Elijah didn't rush to get the toy back, nor did he tell the teacher. Instead, he was cool as a cucumber and just watched and studied Lucas playing with the robot. Later that day, when Lucas sharpened his pencil, Elijah snapped his pencil point off and got in line behind him. He patiently waited for Lucas to finish. Finally, when Lucas turned to go back to his seat, Elijah smirked, stuck his foot out, and tripped him. Elijah was satisfied because Lucas got what was coming to him—justice had been served.

1. How can understanding the different types of anger and aggression help you better help your students?

2. What types of anger or aggression do your students frequently display?

3. What can you do to help the student who internalizes anger?

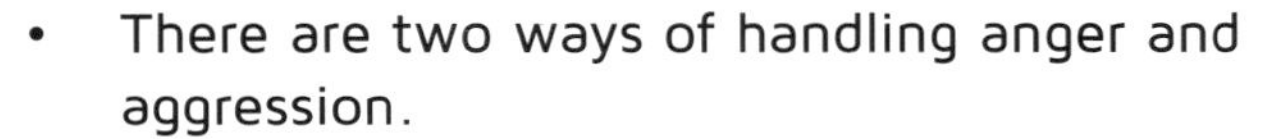

- There are two ways of handling anger and aggression.
- Each type of anger and aggression manifests differently depending on the individual and circumstance.
- Teaching students to self-regulate through helpful self-talk is an effective way to prevent an anger outburst.

5

What Are the Symptoms?

"There are two things a person should never be angry at: what they can help, and what they cannot."

– Plato

We all know how it feels to be angry. What makes one person mad may not even faze another. Also, how we respond to anger can vary from person to person. Anger usually comes with various symptoms, and they can present physically, emotionally, and behaviorally. One of the first steps to managing anger is recognizing the symptoms. This chapter will explore some of the most common features of anger.

Physical Symptoms

Our body's reaction is one of the first indications of anger. When we feel threatened, our body begins to undergo various changes, such as releasing energizing chemicals and hormones. As a result, our heart beats faster, our breathing becomes more rapid and shallow, our muscles flex and tighten, our blood vessels constrict, our hearing becomes more acute, and our vision becomes sharper. This instinctual reaction is known as the fight-or-flight stress response. Unfortunately, when people struggle with chronic anger, they live in this heightened state of alertness. When this happens, it can lead to many health problems, such as high blood pressure, cardiovascular disease, gastrointestinal problems, and even premature death.[24] We can help our students flip the switch of fight or flight by walking through some simple questions, because odds are, in most cases, they aren't in physical danger. Here are a few questions to help your students work through:

1. Am I in physical danger or just mad?
2. Do I need to get all worked up, or can I give this one a pass?
3. What can I do right now to get back in control? (For example, take some slow, deep breaths, go for a walk and get some fresh air, or put down my phone and stop watching how others are responding.) The words we use in our minds can help rile us up or calm us down.

Some physical cues let us know when our fight-or-flight stress response has been activated, and these include:

- Headaches
- Muscle tightness
- Stomach problems
- Rapid heartbeat
- Tensing jaws
- Grinding teeth
- Squinting eyes
- Breathing heavily
- Sweating
- Shaking
- Clenching fists

Emotional Symptoms

Anger can also take an emotional toll on our wellbeing. When we get triggered, it's not uncommon to feel a surge of intense emotions, such as persistent irritability, anxiety, and even rage. You likely know someone who "wears what they are feeling on their sleeves," meaning they display their emotions. It's not uncommon to "walk on eggshells" around these people because you know any little thing may set them off.

Far too often, chronically angry people struggle with relationships because others are afraid of them. You can probably think of a student or two that fits this description, and sadly, you may even know a couple of adults. We have to teach our students to cool their jets in order to have meaningful relationships in their lives. The following are some common emotional symptoms experienced by people who struggle with anger.

- Depression
- Frustration
- Guilt
- Resentment
- Shame
- Stress
- Feeling of being overwhelmed

Behavioral Symptoms

Once the emotions have taken over, behaviors are soon to follow. What we do when we are angry will determine the consequences of our actions. With problematic anger, there are usually hefty consequences to pay. Here are some of the behavioral symptoms most commonly associated with anger:

- Sarcasm
- Pacing
- Physical aggression (punching, hitting, pushing, etc.)
- Raising their voice
- Crying
- Cursing
- Confrontation
- Threatening
- Hurting others
- Harming self
- Using substances

Symptoms of Anger Reference Guide

Symptoms of Anger RECOGNIZING THE CUES		
Physical	**Emotional**	**Behavioral**
• Headaches	• Depression	• Sarcasm
• Muscle Tightness	• Frustration	• Pacing
• Stomach Problems	• Guilt	• Physical Aggrression
• Rapid Heartbeart	• Resentment	• Raising Their Voice
• Tensing Jaws	• Shame	• Crying
• Grinding Teeth	• Stress	• Cursing
• Breathing Heavy	• Overwhelmed	• Confrontational

Try This!

What are your anger symptoms? Fill out the following chart to identify how you physically, emotionally, and behaviorally respond to anger. You can also do this activity with other emotions and feelings in mind, such as stress and anxiety.

Symptoms of Anger RECOGNIZING YOUR CUES		
Physical	**Emotional**	**Behavioral**
• ______________	• ______________	• ______________
• ______________	• ______________	• ______________
• ______________	• ______________	• ______________
• ______________	• ______________	• ______________
• ______________	• ______________	• ______________
• ______________	• ______________	• ______________
• ______________	• ______________	• ______________

A Student's Story

A sweat broke out across Jared's brow. He tightly clenched his fists, and his jaws ached from the tension. His breathing was shallow, and his face was flushed. Every vein in his body felt as though it was popping out of his skin. His heart was pounding out of his chest. His thoughts were racing faster than a horse in the Kentucky Derby. All he could see was red. Jared was beyond angry—he was furious. The one thing he hated was being accused of something he didn't do. It happened at home with his younger siblings snitching on him, and now, he had to come to school and get the same BS from his teachers? No way, no how! How dare Ms. Jenkins accuse him of cheating on a test! And to top it off, she accused him in front of the whole class. How humiliating. Jared stood over six feet tall and glowered down into the eyes of five-foot-tall Ms. Jenkins. "Let me tell you what you can do with your stupid test..." he stated firmly, sprinkling in some explicative language. He threw the exam at her and stormed out of the class, slamming his fist against the lockers on his way down the hall.

QUESTIONS to CONSIDER

1. What are some common physical symptoms you see with angry youth?
2. What are some common emotional symptoms that you see with angry youth?
3. What are some common behavioral symptoms that you see with angry youth?
4. How will understanding the signs and symptoms help you work with angry youth?
5. How will differentiating between physical, emotional, and behavioral symptoms deepen your understanding of anger?

KEY POINTS

- As professionals working with youth, we must teach our students to recognize their thoughts and feelings and exercise control over their actions.
- Physically, chronic levels of anger can take a toll on our health.
- Emotionally, anger can impact how we think about ourselves and relate with others. It can also negatively affect our relationships.
- Behaviorally, anger can be unhealthy and lead to hefty consequences.

6 Integrating Culturally Inclusive Practices

"Usually, when people are sad, they don't do anything. They cry over their condition. But when they get angry, they bring about a change."

~ Malcolm X

Anger is deeply embedded into our culture. When we fail to see the systemic and generational factors that may be affecting behaviors, we fail to address what's impacting our students' decisions. This chapter will explore cultural and systemic factors that play into anger, rage, and aggression. We'll see how different cultures display and express anger and rage, and we'll learn how to take multicultural differences into account when developing anger management interventions.

When we fail to see the systemic and generational factors that may be affecting behaviors, we fail to address what's impacting our students' decisions.

What Is Culture?

There are many definitions of culture, but the Center for Advance Research on Language Acquisition seems to have encapsulated one of the most widely accepted ones: "Culture is shared patterns of behaviors and interactions, cognitive constructs and understanding that are learned by socialization."[25] The word *culture* is derived from the Latin word *colere*, which means to tend to the earth and grow, or cultivation and nurture. Our world is made up of a beautiful cultural tapestry, and woven into each fabric of our being is our heritage, traditions, religion, and the communities in which we reside. Culture is not fixed, but it's fluid, constantly moving and shifting.

Some patterns that shape our culture include:

- Beliefs and thoughts
- Customs and traditions
- Expressions of communication
- Perceptions on roles and relationships
- Styles of communicating and interacting
- Values

Some dimensions that make up our culture include:

- Age
- Gender/Sexual Identity
- Race/Ethnicity
- Language
- Religion/Spirituality
- Socioeconomic status

Try This!

Think about how your culture has shaped you. What creates your cultural tapestry? What are the patterns in your upbringing that influence who you are today? For example, what are common traditions, rituals, or customs ingrained in your story? What dimensions of your life stand out most in your identity? What role does age, gender, religion or spirituality, socioeconomic status, or ethnicity play in your life?

Culture, Anger, and Aggression

Emotions are a source of motivation for how we behave, and as a means of keeping social order, our culture often deems how we should manage our emotions. There are three distinct cultural variations associated with anger: holding it in, controlling it, and letting it out.[26] There are also differences between those from individualistic and collectivist societies. For example, individualistic societies display their anger more, but collectivist societies tend to mask their anger.[27] These differences are due to the display rules that guide what is considered appropriate ways to show emotions. In one study, for example, students in Japan reported their anger was toward strangers and not friends, as not to disrupt peer harmony; however, US and European students would get angry with peers. Their anger was more directed toward their personal relationships.[28]

Many studies have focused on the differences between men and women in anger, rage, and aggression. For example, reactive aggression has been shown to be more acceptable with males than females in given cultural groups.[29] Across cultures, the direct expression of anger and aggression tends to be more accepted in men than women. For example, it has been suggested that in American society, women are socialized to see the direct expression of anger as a harmful threat to relationships, which can lead to social rejection.[30] Thus, culture plays a role in what we deem are acceptable and unacceptable expressions of anger.

When you think about your students, think about how cultural factors and expectations may be impacting their behavior. We know this plays out in schools because research has shown that males reportedly show more physical aggression resulting in disciplinary infractions.[31] So the next time you are working with an angry student, try to understand the big picture of where their anger is coming from; look at all the dimensions of who they are, taking into account their culture.

Generational Impacts

We tend to pass on, often inadvertently, our trauma to those we love. Apply this statement to the concept of culture. If you think of your parents' or families' hardships, you'll be able to see how generational experiences can affect life today. For example, my mother grew up in extreme poverty, and to this day, I can see where her experiences affect me. When I was a child, she would always buy my sister's and my clothes too big because we'd get more wear out of them as we continued to grow, and that came from her own experiences where clothes had to last. Also, most of our clothes were on sale or off the clearance rack. To this day, I still have the mindset that I can't pay full price for something. My mother's growing up in poverty has been ingrained in me. And guess what? I am unintentionally passing a degree of this mindset onto my children. When my daughter goes into a store, she knows to head to the back first because that's where the sales racks hide. My mother's necessity came from survival; mine comes from what I was taught throughout childhood. Perhaps in your own story, you can see where the experiences of your family's history have been passed on to you too.

Now switch gears from your own experiences and think about your students'. For example, think about a parent who has been oppressed, faced extreme injustice, and has realized that authority figures don't protect but instead hurt them. Imagine fighting to get food stamps just to put food in the house, or worse, not getting the medical care your child needs because of lack of money and transportation. Over time, wouldn't you get angry that you can't get your child the medicine they need? Here's something else to consider: someone who has experienced sexual trauma and then has a child of their own. How do you think that child's upbringing will be affected by their parent's adverse experiences? What about racism? Think about generations upon generations of oppression and discrimination and how that affects children today. Bottom line, our family's past experiences are also part of our experiences in some form.

Bottom line, our family's past experiences are also part of our experiences in some form.

Culturally Inclusive Practices

You've heard the saying "seeing the world through a different lens," which essentially means changing your perspective to see something from another angle. Inevitably, you've worked with some angry and aggressive kids. But how much time have you spent exploring how their environment and culture may be contributing to their anger?

For example, think about how oppression, systemic injustice, and microaggressions may play into their anger, rage, and aggression. Using culturally inclusive practices allows us to work from our students' worldviews and not from our own.

A Student's Story

Keenan was in seventh grade and would frequently get into fights. He would go from a 0 to a 10 in a nanosecond. And the one thing that really irritated him was if he was wrongfully accused of something he didn't do. I spent an entire year getting to know Keenan. He was what some would call a frequent flyer. I would ask about home, friends, and school during our time together. I found out that he was the oldest, living in a single-parent home. Unlike most of his peers, he couldn't stay after school for clubs or sports because he had to go home and help his younger siblings. His father wasn't a part of his life, and the family struggled financially.

He remembered being picked on and even beat up in elementary school for his appearance and what he wore. That's when he first felt "less than" (his words) his peers, and that justifiably angered him. Together, we explored how his being picked on impacted how he behaved. And how what was underlying his anger was hurt from being picked on and missing his dad and not getting to connect with his peers because of his responsibilities at home. When Keenan connected the dots to what made him so angry, his behavior started improving. Sometimes a little self-awareness can go a long way.

Several years later, I had a colleague reach out to me because Keenan had written in an assignment about when he learned to manage his anger, and it was all about those times we connected—the times that I listened to his story and helped him connect those dots from his past into his present.

1. What does it mean to be a culturally inclusive educator?
2. How can you incorporate culture in your current role?
3. How can a parent or caregiver's cultural experiences impact their child's life?

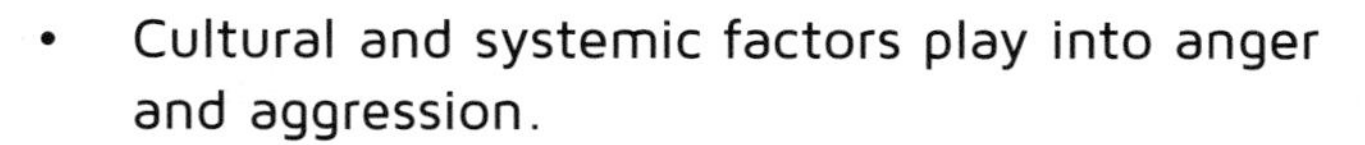

- Cultural and systemic factors play into anger and aggression.
- Society deems appropriate behavior, and these expectations are referred to as display rules.
- Culturally competent educators understand the school community and individual students' diverse cultures and worldviews and can create and tailor interventions that consider their students' culture.
- Anger is best understood by exploring the triggering event and all contributing factors such as microaggressions, disparity, racism, marginalization, oppression, and social-political injustice.
- Culture may very well play into anger, rage, and aggression.

7 Anger Across Childhood and Adolescence

"Anger is an acid that can do more harm to the vessel in which it is stored than to anything on which it is poured."

– Mark Twain

During childhood, anger and aggressive behavior are considered a natural part of the developmental process. However, the way we expect a two-year-old to act when angry is very different from how we expect a teenager to behave. For example, we could see two-year-olds throwing themselves onto the floor kicking and screaming, but if a sixteen-year-old showed those behaviors, we would be very concerned. In this chapter, we'll look at anger through a developmental lens and learn what is appropriate at each phase.

Toddlers and Preschoolers

Biting, crying, hitting, kicking, and screaming sound familiar? These are common ways toddlers and preschoolers react when something does not go their way, and we expect it from them. Unfortunately, young children are impulsive, and they have limited means to express how they feel, so they show us. Too often, acting out is the only way to let us know something is wrong.

During this young phase, aggression often peaks by age two and then gradually decreases by age five. At this age, youth begin to use their words to communicate their wants and needs. However, if a child is developmentally delayed, they may continue to use their behavior as a form of expression.

When working with children in this phase, it's essential to redirect their behaviors toward something more acceptable. For example, if two kids are in a tug-of-war match over the same toy, you may redirect the child's attention by showing them a more appealing and exciting toy. As they get older, you can teach them how to express their thoughts and feelings and find more peaceful solutions by using words. Learning to communicate healthily sets the stage for how children will respond to upsetting situations as they mature.

School-Age Children

As children get older and go to school, they may continue to display some of the same behaviors they did in preschool, like playing too rough, but in time they will begin to grow out of this phase. Children begin to develop friendships during school, so a whole new host of behavioral disruptions may occur, such as bullying, fighting, and teasing. Also, school-age children have a strong desire to be good at something, and they thrive on positive encouragement and support. Their self-esteem is being shaped and molded, and they will carry a piece of this developing self-image with them throughout their lives.

When working with school-age students, it's vital to help them navigate anger-provoking situations. When conflict arises, it's best to deal with it as soon as possible. But make sure the child is calm so you can reason with them. I, personally, like to use feeling charts to help young children identify what they are feeling. The internet has many variations of these charts. So, with a simple search, you can find one that you prefer to use with your students. Emotional scaling is another great technique to use with these kids. You can find anger thermometers on the internet that have numbers showing increasing intensity. There are even visual emoticon scales that are a great way to get information from your student. I also like to role-play through situations to see how they respond and coach them with different, more effective ways to handle the upsetting situation.

Adolescents

As children get older, they get physically more robust, and if they are still using aggression to handle their anger, that can be problematic. In adolescence, students may use physical or verbal aggression to express themselves. Peer conflict may continue to increase with students who didn't learn how to communicate their anger effectively when they were younger. These students may not know how to gain peer acceptance without using force or intimidation. They may also struggle to interpret body language. Their poor social skills only exacerbate their anger.

Angry youth need to be heard, not listened to. They need to be taught how to communicate how they are feeling, and they need to learn how to recognize when they are getting angry and, more importantly, how to calm down. Here are some great ways to help an angry teen cool down.

- Create a playlist of their favorite go-to songs that will help them relax.
- Hit a heavy bag instead of a person.
- Pound it out on the pavement (aka the track with a couple of laps).

As you work with these teens, think back to the toddler who threw a fit and wasn't consistently taught to redirect their behavior appropriately. Think about the school-age child whose parents told them they were "good for nothing," and as a result, they struggled to make friends, leaving them feeling mad, worthless, and all alone. But, most importantly, please think of the missed teachable moments these kids experienced throughout their lives. Now they are at your doorstep, bigger and stronger. Yet, inside they are still a child longing to be taught what to do with the intense anger.

A Student's Story

I remember Brady walking into my office one time, shaking with anger. He told me that if another student did not shut his mouth, he would shut it for him. Based on Brady's body language, there was no way that I was going to ask him to sit down. I could tell that he was a walking bomb waiting to explode. But I knew that if the other student were to cross Brady's path, he would carry through with his promise.

Brady and I took a little field trip to the weightlifting room. In the back of the room, one of the physical education teachers was working in his office and watched as I got Brady some boxing gloves and tossed them to him. I told him to put them on and pointed to the heavy bag, saying, "It's all yours." Brady looked at me in dismay. "Seriously?" he asked. I nodded my head yes, and he began to punch the heavy bag. Each punch was more forceful than the previous one. I remember my colleague looking at me from his office, just shaking his head at the force Brady used to punch the bag. For about fifteen minutes, Brady threw crosses, hooks, and jabs. By the time he finished, he was breathless and dripping with sweat. As he took off the gloves, he looked me in the eye and said, "Thanks, I needed that."

As for me, this was a win-win. Brady was able to release some steam, and I was able to turn an intense situation into a teachable moment. I was able to show my student a less destructive way to work out anger. When he had entered my office, I recognized he needed a physical outlet, and as a result, I provided a safe one for him.

QUESTIONS to CONSIDER

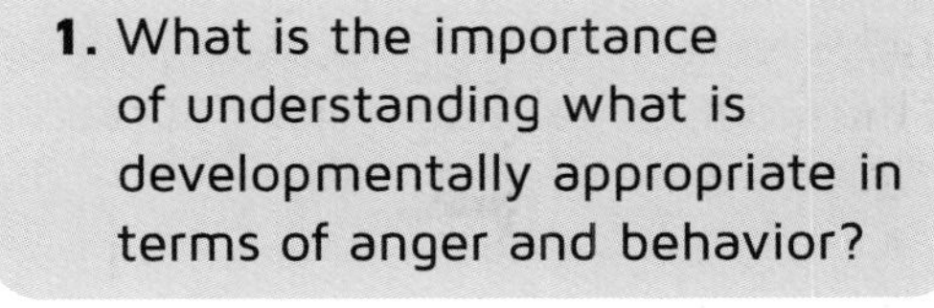

1. What is the importance of understanding what is developmentally appropriate in terms of anger and behavior?

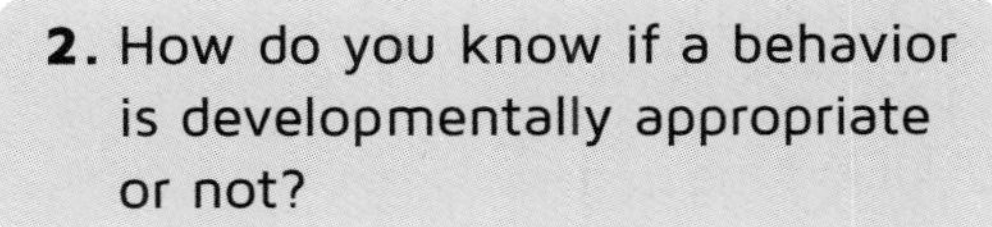

2. How do you know if a behavior is developmentally appropriate or not?

3. What are some ways you can help students identify and communicate their feelings?

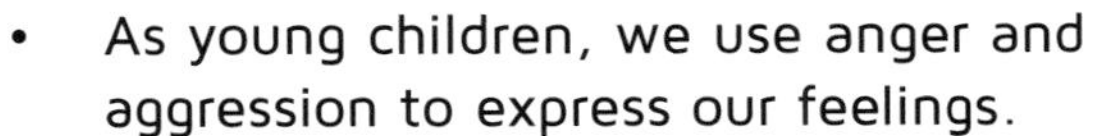

- As young children, we use anger and aggression to express our feelings.

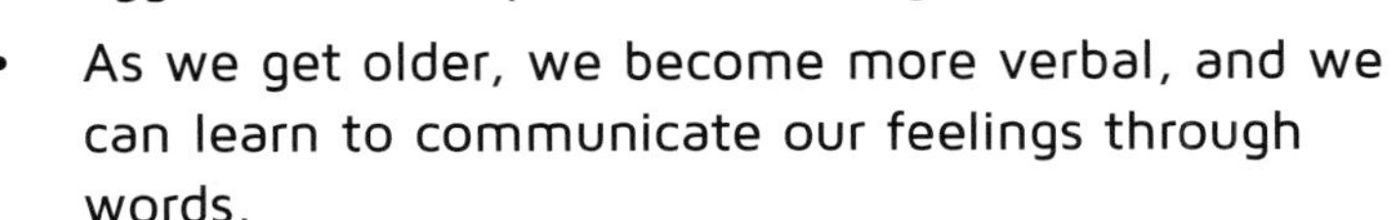

- As we get older, we become more verbal, and we can learn to communicate our feelings through words.
- Seek out teachable moments to show your students healthy ways to work through anger.

Self-Regulating and Managing Anger and Aggression

"The truth about rage is that it only dissolves when it is heard and understood, without reservation."

~ Carl Rogers

As you read in the last chapter, children cope with anger differently based on their age. You wouldn't expect the same behaviors from a preschooler as you would a teen. We need to know evidence-based strategies that are appropriate at various phases of development. Most of the strategies used in this book are derived from behavioral frameworks, cognitive behavioral therapy, social learning theory, and a social information processing framework by understanding how youth encode the information.[32] Over the years, these theoretical modalities effectively treat anger and aggression. Throughout this book, you have been introduced to ways to help angry students, and in this chapter, we will cover research-driven strategies to help you support your angry students.

Preschoolers

Angry preschoolers' reactions can range from crying to a full-out meltdown. At this age, emotions and feelings run the show. These children lack impulse control and struggle to identify their feelings and express them verbally. Their primary mode of communication is through behavior. Preschoolers also struggle to read facial expressions and may misinterpret social cues. These children have only been in the world for forty-eight months or less, so interpreting nonverbal language is learned.

Five Strategies for Helping an Angry Preschooler

In a previous chapter, we discussed redirecting behavior and teaching preschoolers to recognize their feelings. Here are some other ways you can help young children self-manage their anger. *Please note that some of these strategies can be adapted to meet older students' developmental needs.*

1. **Engage in play.** Play therapy is a great way to help young children express their emotions. Through play, you can teach preschoolers to use words for how they feel. For example, while playing, if your preschooler hits you, you can say something like, "Ouch, that hurts, and it makes me sad when you hit me." You are modeling appropriate ways to express and communicate emotions. Teaching children through play can be very instrumental in helping them learn alternate ways to handle stressful situations.

2. **Create a calm space.** Make a safe space for children to go to calm down. Make the space a relaxing one by playing light music, turning on soft light, and having some bean bag chairs on the floor or a comfortable place to sit. By no means should this space be the same space used for disciplinary action, or it will lose its effectiveness. Instead, it needs to be a place that children can go to soothe themselves. Teaching them self-soothing at an early age can help them better regulate emotions when they get older.

3. **Identify feelings and use words.** Once your preschooler is in a calmer place, get down on their level and talk about what happened. Normalize anger by letting them know you get angry too. And share with them what you do to calm down when you're angry. Also, have them identify how anger makes them feel on the inside. There are a lot of diagrams of the body on the

internet. Choose one that's developmentally geared toward the preschool age and have them color the spaces they feel anger on the body and discuss what they can do when they start to feel that place on their body react to anger.

4. **Provide an outlet.** Some kids need to scream and hit. Make sure they have an outlet to express themselves. For example, take them outside and tell them to let it out and shout! If they need to blow off more steam, let them run around or give them a pillow to punch. This is a prime time to teach them that feeling angry is okay, and there are appropriate ways to release it. Have them share ways that they think are okay to release their anger too, and they may come up with a better way than you do!

5. **Read a book or watch a short video clip.** Age-appropriate books and videos are great tools to help kids see other characters work through similar upsetting situations. This strategy allows the child to step back from their problem and see it from another perspective, creating a powerful teachable moment. It's great to create an online folder in which you have already vetted some of these resources, so they are at your fingertips when you need them.

School-Age Children

As children get older and go to school, they may continue to display some of their preschool behaviors, but with time they most likely grow out of behaviors and opt for more age-appropriate ones. So, that means that how you address a school-age child's anger would be different from what you do to help a preschooler. However, the following are some additional strategies you can use with children this age.

Five Strategies for Helping an Angry School-Age Child

1. **Know the signs.** Talk about their anger warning signs. You can use handouts with hollow road signs and have them fill out their warning signs to recognize getting angry. Explain that our bodies show us signs of happiness, sadness, and even anger. Process how their body feels when they feel emotions other than anger. I like to use happy and sad emotions because they are easy for people to explain. So a child may say when they are happy, they smile a lot and giggle. When describing sadness, they may say they frown and cry. Give them a lot of affirmation as they share how they express their emotions with you. Then turn the focus to anger and have them tell you what they do when they are angry. Have them tell you how their body feels when they are mad. Next, ask them what makes them angry and how they behave when they get furious. Again, worksheets are a great way to help students work through what's going on inside their heads and see it on paper.

2. **Use visualization.** Artwork is a great way to help kids work through their emotions. Teach them how to use mental imagery as a calming tool. For example, have them imagine any place in the world they'd like to go. Then, ask them to describe this place in detail. It's not uncommon for children to bring up popular places, their family vacations, grandparents' homes, or places they've seen on TV. Next, have them close their eyes and go to their special place. Afterward, ask them how they are feeling after their imaginary trip. Last, have them draw a picture of their special place or create a collage using pictures from magazines or the internet. Tell the student to put the picture in a readily accessible place to go there any time they need to take a mental break.

3. **Focus, focus.** Pulling an angry child into the present moment can be a challenge, but when children can mentally focus on the here and now, they will, by default, calm down. Here are

some ways to ground an angry child. First, have them find an object in their environment that begins with each letter of the alphabet, beginning with the letter A . Another option is assigning them an object to focus on, like a pencil. Then, have them pay close attention to the color and texture and describe it to you. You may even choose to look around the room for other objects the same color. Although this may not seem like you're doing much, you are engaging them in an evidence-based process known as a grounding that helps them reconnect to the present moment while mentally distracting them from what's making them angry.

4. **Teach healthy self-talk.** The way we talk to ourselves can affect how we feel about ourselves. For example, if we call ourselves "stupid" each time we don't do well on a test, then odds are we won't go into the test feeling confident. However, if we tell ourselves, "That was hard; I'll do better next time," then we'll go in feeling we have another shot at doing well. First, find out what words your students say to themselves by having them write down the common unhelpful words and phrases they use. Next, spin it around and rework the words and phrases into a more helpful statement. Did you know that healthy self-talk has been associated with emotional resilience and positive self-esteem? I often tell students that if they wouldn't say it to close friends, they shouldn't say it to themselves.

5. **Engage in role-playing anger-provoking situations.** For example, how often have you asked a child a question only to get the response of "I don't know"? Well, in truth, they may not know how to put what happened into words, or perhaps they just reacted impulsively and didn't know the why behind their behavior. I like to provide true-to-life scenarios and have students work through them with me in these situations. This technique promotes higher-order thinking, and it helps you see where your student needs help with processing through situations, responding, and coping.

Adolescents

Teens are prone to unpredictability and moodiness. Unfortunately, the intensity of some of those feelings can come at a high price. During the adolescent years, youth seek independence from their parents, and developing relationships with peers are focused more on acceptability and appearance—not to mention the profound changes that puberty brings about physically and psychologically. These elements can create a perfect storm for teens who already struggle with intense emotions, such as anger and rage. The following are some strategies to help an angry teen.

Four Strategies for Helping an Angry Adolescent

1. **Listen.** Teens want to be heard. When they are angry, stop and listen. Work to understand what happened from their perspective. Remember, their perception is reality, and trying to convince them differently will only fan the flames. Attentive listening will not only help your student open up and process their feelings, but it will also help establish rapport between you and your student.

   You can show active listening by following these simple steps:

   ✓ **Be fully present and engaged.** Face the student when they are talking with you, and give the student your undivided attention.

   ✓ **Use silence.** Don't feel as though you must fill space with words. There is a lot of power in silence. Silence allows space to process thoughts and begin to understand them more deeply. A slow and steady pace is what it takes to help your students work through their intense emotions.

   ✓ **Give minimal encouragers.** For example, "I see," "Uh-huh," "Okay," and "Tell me more" can encourage your student to open up and share at a deeper level.

   ✓ **Give nonverbal affirmations.** Nod your head in agreement to show your attentiveness.

- ✓ **Clarify.** Ask open-ended questions to make sure you understand what your student is saying.
- ✓ **Summarize.** At the end of the conversation, condense what your student said in a few short sentences to show you got what they are saying.

2. **Teach mindful decompression strategies.**

   Anger is an intense energy-producing emotion that needs some outlet to escape. Imagine anger as a pressure cooker that has reached its maximum temperature. As the pressure builds, it sounds like it's going to explode at any moment unless that steam is released. Our job is to help teach students skills to release that steam in healthy ways. One way to do that is by practicing some of the following decompression strategies.

   - ✓ **Breathing.** Take slow breaths through the nose and out of the mouth. I often have youth imagine they are blowing up a balloon in the stomach by inhaling deeply and then steadily deflating it as they exhale. To throw some imagery in, I ask them to tell me the color of their balloon to visualize it when they are breathing in and out. Also, if you have a pinwheel, you can have students blow the pinwheel and watch it turn as they are practicing deep breathing. The spinning colors add another dimension of distraction and relaxation. Plus, it gives them something else to do and doesn't feel awkward sitting there and breathing with you.
   - ✓ **Meditation.** The goal here is to move your student out of their headspace. Have them close their eyes or gaze at a picture and focus on their breathing. Have them notice how their body feels as they are beginning to relax. Tell them to take the issue that's troubling them and move it to the background so they can fully be present in the moment. Each time their mind tries to wander back to the problem, they call it back to the present. Tell them that meditation is a great way to bring clarity to the situation by moving them away from the troubling situation for a few minutes. I often describe anger as a hamster in a wheel. It just spins and spins and goes nowhere. If we can get our students out of the wheel, they may see their situation from a different view

and, better yet, come up with a more productive solution to the problem, rather than just spinning their wheels. As easy as meditation looks on paper, I assure you it is no simple task because when stressed or angry, our minds tend to race, and we become tunnel-visioned. This skill needs to be practiced regularly, like ten to fifteen minutes per day.

- ✓ **Progressive Muscle Relaxation (PMR)**. In PMR, have students tense each muscle group without straining, beginning at their feet and ending with their head. Next, have them reverse by releasing the tension starting with the head and ending at the feet. This activity helps relax both the mind and the body. I remember learning this technique in grade school, but I remember the feeling of being like a rag doll. I even remember my teacher telling us that we should feel like a rag doll at the end of the exercise, our muscles so relaxed that we just flopped. That was many years ago, and I still remember learning PMR. It just shows how powerful these simple techniques can be and how they can stick with us well into adulthood.
- ✓ **Grounding.** The grounding process is to bring students out of their thoughts and into the present moment by tapping into their surroundings. It's somewhat like meditation but has an intentional focus. For example, the 5-4-3-2-1 method focuses on five things they see, four things they feel, three things they hear, two things they smell, and one thing they can taste. Like meditation, the more practice students have at pulling themselves into the present, the stronger the skills will become.

3. **From the outside looking in.** A great way to help teens cope with anger is to explore their thoughts and feelings from an "outside looking in" perspective. I like to think of this technique as peering into a window of your life and becoming an observer to what's happening. You can even have students be a narrator of their own stories. Sometimes I'll ask teens to pretend they are another teen who witnessed everything because it takes

them outside of themselves to see the situation from another perspective.

4. **Use symbolism.** Teens seem to like using symbolism and meaning. I once had a student tell me that when she got angry, she went into the garage and nailed nails into a wooden board, with each pound of the hammer reflecting something she was angry at. Although you may not have nails and hammers readily accessible for your student to swing in your office, you can use other techniques. For example, have your student write down everything that has made them angry. Encourage them to let it all out and not hold back. Next, pull over a trash can and tell them to release that anger by ripping what's on that paper into shreds, and as they pull each strip from the paper, imagine it letting the anger go.

A Student's Story

Emma was having a tough day at school. Her friends ignored her at recess, and no one would tell her why they wouldn't talk to her. So, when the class was in line at the water fountain, Emma "accidentally" bumped Sophia's back so that her face went into the stream of water. "Hey!" Sophia yelled loud enough for Mr. Ammons to turn and see the water dripping from Sophia's face. Before a fight broke out, Mr. Ammons had Emma walk to the counselor's office and cool down. As Emma walked into the familiar office, she plopped down on her usual bean bag chair and sighed loudly. Mr. James, the counselor, got out of his chair and plopped into the bean bag chair across from Emma. "Tough day?" he asked. "You have no idea!" Emma exclaimed. "Want to talk about it?" Mr. James asked. "No." Emma snapped back. "Okay, well, how about we talk about something else first until you're ready? Sound good?" Emma didn't reply but looked at Mr. James and shrugged her shoulders. Mr. James knew that Emma would eventually get around to what was bothering her, but it took time for her to sort through it in her mind. Mr. James had Emma practice a few slow, steady breaths and then had her look at a large jungle picture he had hanging in his office. He had Emma name as many animals as she could in the picture. Emma always liked visiting Mr. James. He helped her feel better. Before long, Emma just started talking about her day, and Mr. James didn't even need to start the conversation because he let Emma set the pace. After Emma shared, Mr. James realized that Emma's behavior was out of fear of losing her friends because they weren't nice to her anymore. She failed to see that her behaviors weren't getting her any closer to keeping those friends but instead were pushing them further away.

1. What strategies have you tried in the past to help an angry student?
   a. What was least successful?
   b. What was most successful?

2. What new strategy do you want to try to support your upset student?

3. What would you do differently to help an angry preschooler versus an angry teen, even if the teen is showing some of the same behaviors as a preschooler?

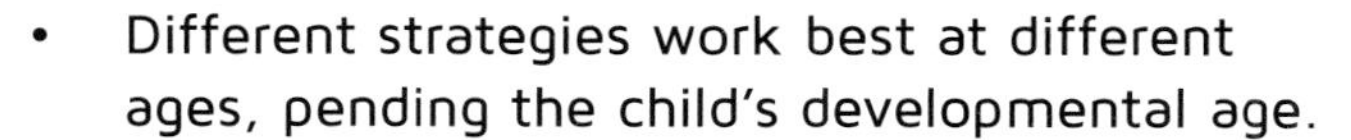

- Different strategies work best at different ages, pending the child's developmental age.
- Some of the strategies for each development phase can be modified to work with older children.
- As an educator, when working with a student with anger issues, we must understand they haven't grasped the necessary skills to regulate and manage their anger effectively.

9 De-escalating Anger, Rage, and Aggression

"No one heals himself by wounding another."

~ St. Ambrose of Milan

Have you ever had to intervene and de-escalate an angry, rageful, or aggressive student? If so, you know you really must handle the student with kid gloves. However, some helpful tactics work in calming an angry student. In this chapter, we'll explore some de-escalation tactics that you can use the next time you're working with an angry, rage-filled, or aggressive student.

Amygdala Hijack

Understanding how to calm an angry person begins with understanding the neurological process that occurs in the amygdala, a collection of cells near the base of the brain. The amygdala is a part of the brain's limbic system. There are two, one on each side of the brain. When we feel endangered, our amygdala pulls the fire alarm and sends a message to our frontal lobes. Our frontal lobes try to problem solve and determine the severity of the danger. When we aren't in imminent danger, our frontal lobes can usually reason with our amygdala and call it a false alarm. It's when we are worked up that problems can occur. Our amygdala will override the frontal lobes and trigger our fight-or-flight stress response if we are angry. Daniel Goleman referred to this process as the "amygdala hijack." [33]

When the amygdala takes over, logic can cease to exist, and behaviors are difficult to control. This hijack process is why it's hard to reason with an angry person and why it's best to allow a cool-down period before having them rehash what caused their anger. With proper de-escalation techniques, we can teach students how to turn off the blaring alarms and let their frontal lobes be the voice of reason.

Five De-escalation Tactics Every Educator Should Know

1. **Remain calm.** The goal of de-escalation is to build rapport with your agitated student quickly. If you act nervous or stressed, your student can pick up your feelings and it can cause them to feel unsafe, which may escalate their anger. You can help a student regain control by showing them you are calm and confident. Remain as neutral as possible, relax your posture, and don't move around as it can intensify the situation. Let your calm, relaxed voice guide you through the situation. How you react to an angry student may help determine the outcome of their behavior.
2. **Listen.** Angry students can speak disrespectfully and may even use a colorful vocabulary to express their frustration. Rather than correcting their language, a more productive approach would be to affirm what they are feeling and let them know how upsetting this situation is. Let them know you are there to listen and help them work through this issue. Acknowledging how they feel is one of the most crucial de-escalation tactics that you can use. One of the best questions you can ask an angry student is, "How can I help you?"
3. **Pay attention to the warning signs.** Students often provide behavioral clues that their anger is climbing, and these include:
   - A change in mood or demeanor
   - Moving around more, such as pacing or taking up more proximal space than normal
   - A change in the tone of their voice. For example, listen for sarcasm, harsh undertones, deep and gravelly sounds, threatening, grumbling, or increasing volume when speaking.
   - Uncontrolled body language. Frequently, angry students' gestures become uncontrolled. For example, they may start flailing their

arms, pointing their fingers, shaking, squinting, tapping feet, or balling up their fists.

4. **Create a safer environment.** To decrease the chance of escalation, make sure that you disperse any onlookers. Also, try to make the environment as distraction-free and quiet as possible. Ideally, the location you choose will have a lot of space for movement. Remember, anger is an energy-producing emotion, so having the student sit in a small office is not ideal. It's amazing what a few tweaks in the atmosphere can do to de-escalate an angry student.
5. **Distance yourself physically.** Students who are angry and aggressive may lash out. Be mindful of your space, and unless you need to intervene, do not get too close to the student; they need space. If you infringe on their space, they may feel threatened and become more agitated. Also, do not touch an angry student because they may impulsively retaliate. Make sure that you have the means to exit the situation if you can. In other words, do get pinned behind a desk with the student blocking the door. Listen to your gut. If you don't feel the student is calming down within the first few minutes, stop trying to de-escalate the situation and get assistance. If you keep trying to calm them, it could backfire and cause more of a scene.

Say *This*, Not *That*

1. Some students will have a difficult time communicating their feelings. Asking them to communicate something they don't know how to express will frustrate them more. It's better to focus on their thoughts, not how they are feeling

   Say: "You seem worked up. Let me help you calm down."

   Not: "How are you feeling?"

2. It's not uncommon for students to become rude and even curse when angry. Even though you may see this as a blatant sign of disrespect, you can help the student by letting them know you see them.

Say: "I can see how upsetting this is to you."

Not: "You can't talk like that."

Remember, when the amygdala has been hijacked, students are in reaction mode, and having them rehash what got them angry will only lead to more anger. So it's best to focus on getting the frontal lobes back in control before trying to reason with them and find out what led to their anger, aggression, or rage.

Say: "How can I help you?" or "What has helped you calm down in the past?"

Not: "Tell me everything that just happened."

3. Re-directing behavior can be a challenge, but it's not impossible. It's all in how you go about helping your student express themselves while setting clear boundaries.

   Say: "I am sorry you're so upset. How about we go for a walk and get some fresh air."

   Not: "You need to calm down and stop yelling."

A Student's Story

When students are experiencing an anger episode the last thing you want to do is have them rehash the details of the triggering event. Trust me, this tactic won't de-escalate the situation, but rather it adds fuel to the fire. Take the example of Kyle. Kyle was one of my frequent fliers—the student who was regularly sent to my office, and if he wasn't being sent he was seeking me out. Needless to say, Kyle and I got to know each other pretty well. If a situation occurred at school, I was frequently called in to help Kyle. You may have a similar student who comes to mind.

One day I was at work going about my business when my phone rang , summoning me to the principal's office. Walking in, I saw Kyle seething mad sitting in a cold stare with the principal. I was told Kyle was involved in a physical altercation and had to be pulled off another student.

Honestly, at first glance Kyle didn't look like himself. When angry, we tend to undergo transformations that radiate the message to "back off." The veins were popping out of his neck, and his eyes were narrowed like a predator looking for prey. Kyle's breathing was so heavy I could hear it from across the room. The principal motioned for me to have a seat in a chair next to Kyle's. *Sure, you have a desk between you and him*, I thought. I inched slowly toward the chair and felt like I was walking on egg shells. Sliding into the chair, I could feel the tension and energy radiating off of Kyle. And then the principal did it—he asked that loaded question that set the cannon off. He asked Kyle to tell him everything that happened. I watched Kyle's eyes as they were reliving everything that just happened, and when he started to speak I could tell he was getting worked up even more! Kyle didn't get through a few sentences before jumping to his feet and storming out of the office.

The lesson here is that if you want to de-escalate a situation, put some time and space between the event and the student. Students need to calm down, not rev up. Talking and reasoning can come at a later time. What Kyle needed most was to de-escalate and calm down. When people are consumed with anger, a little space and silence can go a long, long way.

1. After reviewing de-escalation tactics, what area do you believe will be the most challenging for you?
2. How can your ability to remain calm help an angry student?
3. What can you say or do differently when working with a highly agitated student?
4. What tactics have you found to help diffuse anger?

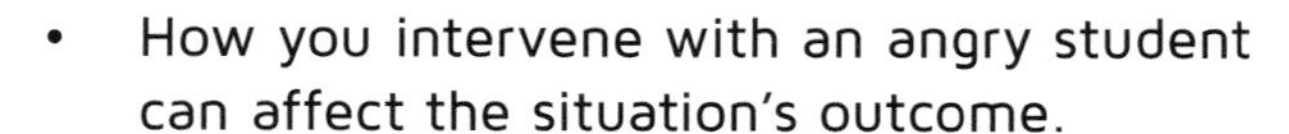

- How you intervene with an angry student can affect the situation's outcome.
- Even if you don't feel equipped to handle the situation, when you model calmness and control, you set the stage for the student to do the same.
- You can help create an environment that helps your student feel safe, which can help de-escalate anger.
- Trust your instincts. Don't keep trying if you cannot de-escalate the student within the first few minutes, as it may be counterproductive. Instead, get assistance and maintain space between yourself and the student. This is for the safety of both you and your student.

10 Supporting Parents and Families

"Love me when I least deserve it because that's when I need it the most."

~ Swedish Proverb

Anger can be taxing on the parent-child relationship. Unfortunately, many parents are at a loss when their child's temper soars out of control, and they feel entirely unequipped for what to do. As a result, they may turn to school officials, like yourself, for support. This chapter will provide you with essential information to help parents better manage their child's anger, rage, and aggression.

Helping Parents

If a parent is seeking out your expertise, they most likely have exhausted all other efforts in curbing their child's temper. They are likely coming to you worried, weary, and worn. But you can assure them that you are here to support them. In my work with parents, I remind myself that most parents are doing the best they can with what they have. This helps me meet them where they are in their parenting. It also helps keep me centered that we have a common mission of helping their child, and by helping them, I am indirectly helping their child. For starters, here are three immediate things to do when a parent seeks out your assistance.

1. Take the time to listen and acknowledge their struggle with their child.
2. Affirm the difficulty of their situation.
3. Let them know that you are there to help.

Assessing Anger

Begin by getting information from them about their child's behavior. Asking some basic questions can help you determine the severity of the child's anger and how it affects the home environment. Use the following questions as a tool to help you gain a clearer insight into the child's behavior. I'd recommend putting these questions into a document, having parents fill them out, and then reviewing them in your interview. As needed, request for the parents to expand on any question. The more you understand the child's behavior, the more assistance you'll be able to provide.

Please answer the following questions and provide as much information as possible on your child's problematic behavior.

1. Describe your child's behavior at home?

   ____

   ____

2. What seems to most trigger your child's anger?

   ____

   ____

3. How long has your child's disruptive behavior been occurring?

   ____

   ____

4. Was there a specific event that may have led to your child's behavior?

____

____

5. Has your child's behavior ever been a danger to themself or others?

____

____

6. Has your child's behavior ever led to the destruction of property?

____

____

7. What type of trouble does your child's behavior cause at school?

____

____

8. What type of trouble does your child's behavior cause at home?

____

____

9. Does your child's anger affect their relationships with peers?

____

____

10. Does your child have healthy friendships? *Remember to consider the developmental level with this question. With a five-year-old, their friendships would look different from a teen's.*

____

____

Yes or No Questions:

11. My child ruminates on anger-triggering events.
    Yes___ No___
12. My child has difficulty forgiving those who have done them wrong.
    Yes___ No___
13. My child is in frequent trouble at school and other social settings because of their temper or anger outbursts.
    Yes___ No___
14. My child flies off the handle quickly and is difficult to soothe.
    Yes___ No___
15. My child frequently gets into trouble at home due to anger outbursts.
    Yes___ No___
16. My child loses friends due to anger issues.
    Yes___ No___
17. My child lashes out verbally and physically with anger.
    Yes___ No___
18. My child says troublesome things, verbalizes threats, or writes about or draws disturbing and violent pictures.
    Yes___ No___
19. My child searches for weaponry or other disturbing information on the internet.
    Yes___ No___
20. My child has difficulty letting things go and will frequently bring up the past.
    Yes___ No___

Please expand on the following questions.

21. What efforts have you tried to help calm your child?

    ____

    ____

22. What has worked in the past to calm your child?

____

____

23. What is the most pressing concern that you have about your child's anger?

____

____

24. What would you like to see change with your child's behavior at home in an ideal world? School? Other social settings?

____

____

25. Is there any other information that you believe would help me better understand your child's behavior?

____

____

The above questions are not intended to diagnose nor are they a crystal ball into your child's behaviors. However, your responses can help you pinpoint patterns and themes. For example, do you notice your child often resorts to physical aggression or struggles with peer-to-peer communication? Any commonalities that you detect may help you identify what provokes your child's anger. If you are at your wits' end with your child's behaviors and they are causing a significant problem at home or school, please speak with a school official to learn about community supports and trained professionals who can help your child learn emotional regulation skills.

Managing Anger at Home

The following are some tactics that you can share with parents to help them better manage disruptive behaviors at home.

1. **Remain calm and confident.** Stay calm when your child is having a moment. Use a soothing and confident voice when talking to them. Harsh or angry responses may escalate your child's anger. By remaining calm and confidently in control of the situation, you're modeling—and teaching—your child the type of behavior you expect them to reciprocate.
2. **Identify triggers.** You can decrease angry outbursts by identifying triggering events. For the next few days, track your child's anger. Note the times and events the anger occurred. For example, do most occur in the morning prior to school, when in social situations with friends, or perhaps around mealtime or bedtime? Monitoring anger events can help show if themes are surrounding the disruptive behaviors.

For older students, have them self-monitor their behavior by noting dates, times, triggering events, their anger response, and what they would do differently if anything.

3. **Track anger.** If you are unsure how frequently the anger issues occur, consider tracking the incidents on a chart, a calendar, or a journal. Your tracking system should be kept in a private place. In other words, don't post your chart on the refrigerator or in a common place for all family members to see. We don't want to call attention to your child's undesirable behaviors, but rather work to decrease them. Tracking is for you to identify triggering behaviors and see what does and doesn't work in calming your child. If your child is older or an adolescent, you can have them track their own behaviors, a concept referred to as *self-monitoring*. Examples of working with younger and older children are provided.

The following is an example of what you may want to record with younger children.

Date and Time	What was the triggering event?	What were your child's anger signs during the triggering event?	What were the reactions to the behavior and what was the response?	What would you do differently to help your child calm down?
Example: *Monday 5p.m.*	*Zack was getting ready for soccer practice and couldn't find one of his shoes.*	*Stomping loudly around the house and slamming doors and raising his voice. Blaming his sister for messing with his things.Yelling for help. Ripping clothes out of his closet looking for his shoe.*	*I told him to chill out and stop tearing the house apart and accusing his sister for his irresponsibility. I told him if he didn't find his shoe, then he'd just miss practice.* *When I threatened him it only escalated the situation.*	*I should have gone to him, helped him relax by taking deep breaths, and then retraced his steps from when he last had his shoes. Looking back his anxiety was fueling his anger.* *In the future we will work on preparing the night before rather than waiting until the last minute to get his things together.*

The following is an example of what your older child may include when self-monitoring their behavior.

Date and Time	What happened?	What did you feel?	What did you think?	What did you do?	What were the conse-quences?	What would you do differ-ently?
Example: *Monday 9 a.m.*	*Teacher called on me to answer a question about the weekend's homework that I didn't do.*	*Scared because I didn't want to everyoneto know I didn't do it and get a bad grade.*	*This is stupid. I didn't have time to do the work and if my parents find out I didn't do it they'll flip.*	*Told the teacher to pick someone esle and when she would not let it go, I blamed her for always picking on me and told her to get off my (expletive) case.*	*Principal's office, after school deten-tion,had to call home about the incident, and zero on the assign-ment.*	*Just own up to it. The con-sequence would have been less, had I just said I didn't do the assignment and left it at that.*

4. **Create an Anger Management Plan.** Create a plan to help your child deal with the anger more appropriately. Set up a system to help your child manage disruptive behaviors based on the information you received by creating an anger management plan that includes calm-down strategies to use. For example, perhaps your child needs to take a time-out when angry. So, use a one-word or hand signal to let others know they need to step away from the situation. Please note that stepping away does not mean avoiding. You can cycle back to the event once your child has had some time to collect themselves.

Sample Anger Management Plan

IDENTIFY THE GOAL

I want to:

In their own words have your child tell you what they want to change about their behaviors. Rather than saying "Don't get angry," have them break that down into obtainable tasks because they are human and will get angry. For example, they may work on their anger response like not screaming or breaking things when they get angry.

MONITORING ANGER

On an anger scale of 1 to 10, with 1 being *relaxed and calm* to 10 being *extremely angry*, list your feelings, thoughts, and behaviors at each level of the scale.

SCALING NUMBER	FEELINGS, THOUGHTS, AND BEHAVIORS AT EACH LEVEL
10 (maximum anger)	
9	
8	
7	
6	
5	
4	
3	
2	
1 (minimum anger)	

ANGER SIGNS

This is what I do now when I am angry:

Have your child list their anger signs so they can become aware of how they are responding to an upsetting situation. Examples may include:

- *I raise my voice*
- *I hit things*
- *I slam things*
- *I feel hot*
- *I feel like my heart's beating fast*
- *I clench my teeth*
- *I ball up my fists*
- *I run away*
- *I cry*
- *I call people names*
- *I tear up things*

This is what usually happens when I act that way:

Have your child list the consequences of their above behaviors.

This is what I will do instead:

Have your child list ways to effectively calm down. Unlike the anger tracker, you could print out the list of calming strategies and display it in an accessible place, like the fridge, so your child can refer to it in the heat of the moment. A few examples are provided.

- *Read*
- *Listen to music*
- *Go for a bike ride*
- *Go for a run*
- *Take 10 deep breaths counting to 10 each time*
- *Write down what's bothering me and rip it up*
- *Talk about what's bothering me*
- *Do 30 jumping jacks*
- *Write in a journal*
- *Draw my feelings on a piece of paper*

ACKNOWLEDGING PROGRESS
I will review this plan each week on ________________ for progress and if my behavior has improved I would like to: *Help your child come up ways to celebrate their success. For example, spend some extra time at the park, or have play time with a friend. If your child is older you may have something like pizza from their favorite restaurant, watching a movie together, or hanging out with some friends. The point is to find simple ways to acknowledge their hard work. The real reward is the change in their behavior.*

5. **Teach the basics.** When children are angry, they may be clueless about social rules, like personal space. As a result, they may get in your face, scream at the top of their lungs, or slam things around. These intense behaviors can escalate anger with your child and in yourself. Teach your child to speak in a lower tone and not yell when angry. Teach them to have a few steps between themselves and the person they speak with. Also, teach them to watch how the other person reacts to what they are doing. For example, teach them to watch their body language by not standing with their arms crossed, fists balled up, or chest poked out, as each of these can be considered offensive and create more tension and defensiveness.

Getting More Help

As we explored in chapter 2, some symptoms transcend beyond the scope of anger. These conditions may require professional assistance. If you notice that anger has significantly impaired the child's ability to function at home, school, or other social settings, please help parents locate the necessary resources to help their child. Additional information is provided in the Resource section.

A Student's Story

Mia clenched her fists and let out a blood-curdling scream when her mother told her they would not go to the park that afternoon. Leah, Mia's mom, was exhausted. A newborn baby in the home had contributed to Leah being severely sleep-deprived, and her only reprieve was when

Mia was away at school. She hated to admit it, but she dreaded when Mia got home because that's when chaos erupted. Mia's anger had been escalating ever since the birth of her new brother. Leah had done everything she could think of to curb Mia's disruptive behaviors, including purchasing books, watching videos, and reading blogs on an unruly child, but nothing seemed to help. She was at a complete loss. Mia's behavior was getting so out of control that she even feared for her baby's safety if left in the same room. Mia was in kindergarten, and Leah had hoped that the age gap between her two children would be helpful. She and Mia's father had intentionally planned for Mia to be off to school before having another baby because it would allow individual time for each child. Not to mention, they thought that Mia would be a good age to help her mother with a new baby. But you know what they say about best-laid plans. What they got was not what they bargained for. Sure, Leah hadn't spent as much time with Mia as she did before her brother's birth, but Mia was a big sister, and Leah needed her help—not more problems. That same day, Leah got a call from school, asking her to come in for an appointment. It appeared that Mia's behavior wasn't only affecting life at home but also school.

In Mia's scenario, there are several factors to take into consideration.

1. Mia's age is important to factor into the scenario. Remember, children this age are most likely to express their feelings physically. They throw tantrums, stomp their feet, scream, and cry, to name a few. Young children lack impulse control and immediately act out when they get their way.
2. Consider the triggering events in Mia's life. First, we know this is her first year away from her mom, with the beginning of school and the birth of a new brother. Mia may be feeling pushed out.
3. Think about all of the feelings that Mia may be experiencing. Go beyond the surface of anger and think about other emotions and feelings at the root of her behavior. For example, hurt, fear, and jealousy may be contributing to her behavioral outbursts.

   Although these things may seem obvious to us, it's not uncommon for parents to get so sidetracked by the problematic behavior that they fail to see what lies in front of them.

QUESTIONS to CONSIDER

1. How is the child's behavior impacting the home environment?
2. What strategies have the parents tried to help curb their child's anger?
3. What are the most common triggers to their child's anger?
4. What other feelings are underlying the anger and aggression?
5. What past strategies have been effective in helping their child calm down?

- Angry, rageful, and aggressive children can create a lot of stress in the home and cause strain on the parent-child relationship.
- By the time many parents seek your help, they may have exhausted all other resources.
- You can help parents assess how the anger is impacting the home environment.
- You can help parents understand their child's behavior and support them in helping their child manage anger.

Conclusion

Across the nation, anger is a common problem in schools. Unfortunately, too often, educators are addressing these disruptive and problematic behaviors. As we have discussed throughout this book, many students who lash out with anger, rage, or aggression don't know other ways to release their intense emotions. Their lack of emotional regulation and impulse control creates a perfect storm for behavioral outbursts. Fortunately, as educators, we have a unique opportunity to help our students learn effective coping strategies that are productive and healthy.

Anger is neither good nor bad. It's just an emotion, a universal one at that. Anger isn't the problem and never has been. The problem with anger lies in how it's handled. Far too often, angry children are penalized for their angry behaviors. As a result, they face more disciplinary consequences, peer isolation, and exclusion compared to their peers. We can all agree, none of these are healthy situations for children to thrive.

At the beginning of the book, we discussed how all behavior serves a purpose and that their perception is reality. This is important for us to remember when addressing a child's anger. If we can try to see the issue from their worldview, we can truly design an intervention specific to their needs. Addressing anger is not a one-size-fits-all approach. We must look at the contributing factors to what's causing the anger, and these vary by individual. Too often, an angry child's behaviors are the focus of attention. We fail to go beyond the surface of anger and tap into what's causing the issues. By failing to help our students sort through what's bugging them, we miss golden opportunities to help them.

Teaching our students at an early age to manage their anger and find healthy ways to express it can be a gift that lasts well into adulthood. Anger has been associated with health and relationship problems, and it can have an adverse impact on a person's ability to perform at school, work, and other social settings. By intervening early, we can teach our students that anger isn't the problem, but how they express it may be. Going back to the gentleman who I met at my book signing, by no means do we want our youth sharing a story in their older adulthood about how they had to suffer through broken relationships and health problems to find peace from anger. Instead, let's go to the heart of the matter and teach them where to find their inner peace at an early age, the true gift of a lifetime.

Thank you so much for being interested in helping angry and aggressive youth. And more importantly, thank you for all that you do to enrich the lives of children.

In Peace,

Dr. Raychelle Cassada Lohmann

DOWNLOADABLE RESOURCES

The resources in this book are available for you as a digital download!

Please visit **15minutefocusseries.com** and click this book cover on the page. Once you've clicked the book cover, a prompt will ask you for a code to unlock the activities.

Please enter code:

Anger432

Notes

1. D. Sukhodolsky et al., "Behavioral Interventions for Anger, Irritability, and Aggression in Children and Adolescents," *Journal of Child and Adolescent Psychopharmacology* 26(2016): 58–64, https://doi:10.1089/cap.2015.0120.
2. L. C. Girard et al., "Development of Aggression Subtypes from Childhood to Adolescence: a Group-Based Multi-Trajectory Modelling Perspective," *Journal of Abnormal Child Psychology* 47, no. 5 (2019): 825–38, https://doi: 10.1007/s10802-018-0488-5.
3. F. Keith et al., "Anger, Hostility, and Hospitalizations in Patients with Heart Failure," *Health Psychology* 36, no. 9 (2017): 829–38, https://doi.org/10.1037/hea0000519.
4. Raychelle Lohmann, "Finding Your Inner Peace," *Psychology Today*, July 11, 2014, https://www.psychologytoday.com/us/blog/teen-angst/201407/finding-your-inner-peace.
5. Paul Ekman, *Emotions Revealed: Recognizing Faces and Feelings to Improve Communication and Emotional Life* (St. Martin's Griffin, 2007).
6. C. D. Spielberger, E. C. Reheiser, and S. J. Sydeman, "Measuring the Experience, Expression, and Control of Anger," *Issues in Comprehensive Pediatric Nursing* 18, no. 3 (1995): 207–32.
7. "Mental Health: Strengthening Our Response," World Health Organization, March 30, 2018, https://www.who.int/news-room/fact-sheets/detail/mental-health-strengthening-our-response.
8. R. M. Ghandour et al., "Prevalence and Treatment of Depression, Anxiety, and Conduct Problems in U.S. Children," *The Journal of Pediatrics* 206(2018): 256–67, https://doi.org/10.1016/j.jpeds.2018.09.021.
9. "Mental Health," World Health Organization.
10. "Anxiety and Depression in Children: Get the Facts," Centers for Disease Control and Prevention, March 22, 2021, https://www.cdc.gov/childrensmentalhealth/features/anxiety-depression-children.html.
11. M. Jha et al., "Anger Attacks Are Associated with Persistently Elevated Irritability and Moderate Depressive Disorder," *Psychological Medicine Advance* 51, no. 8 (2020): 1355–63, https://doi.org/10.1017/S0033291720000112.
12. A. N. Kaczkurkin and E. B. Foa, "Cognitive-behavioral Therapy for Anxiety Disorders: an Update on the Empirical Evidence," *Dialogues in Clinical Neuroscience* 17, no. 3 (201): 337–46, https://doi.org/10.31887/DCNS.2015.17.3/akaczkurkin.

13. "Data and Statistics About ADHD," Centers for Disease Control and Prevention, September 23, 2021, https://www.cdc.gov/ncbddd/adhd/data.html.

14. American Psychiatric Association, *Diagnostic and Statistical Manual of Mental Disorders, Fifth Edition* (DSM-5), 2013.

15. "Anxiety and Depression in Children," Centers for Disease Control and Prevention.

16. S. C. Curtin, "State Suicide Rates Among Adolescents and Young Adults Aged 10–24: United States, 2000–2018," Centers for Disease Control and Prevention, September 11, 2020, https://stacks.cdc.gov/view/cdc/93667.

17. American Psychiatric Association, *Diagnostic and Statistical Manual of Mental Disorders*.

18. American Psychiatric Association.

19. American Psychiatric Association.

20. American Psychiatric Association.

21. N. R. Crick and K. A. Dodge, "Social Information-Processing Mechanisms in Reactive and Proactive Aggression," *Child Development* 67(1996): 993–1002, https://doi:10.1111/j.14678624.1996.tb01778.x.

22. Crick and Dodge.

23. Crick and Dodge; K. A. Dodge J. Godwin, and the Conduct Problems Prevention Research Group, "Social-Information-Processing Patterns Mediate the Impact of Preventive Intervention on Adolescent Antisocial Behavior," *Psychological Science* 24 (2013): 456–65, https://doi 10.1177/0956797612457394.

24. Keith et al., "Anger, Hostility, and Hospitalizations in Patients with Heart Failure."

25. Center for Advanced Research on Language Acquisition, "What Is Culture?", April 9, 2019, https://carla.umn.edu/culture/definitions.html.

26. P. B. Smith et al., "Cultural Variations in the Relationship Between Anger Coping Styles, Depression, and Life Satisfaction," *Journal of Cross-Cultural Psychology* 47, no. 3 (2016): 441–56.

27. D. Matumoto et al., "Mapping Expressive Differences Around the World: The Relationship Between Emotional Display Rules and Individualism Versus Collectivism," *Journal of Cross-Cultural Psychology* 39 (2008): 55–74.

28. K. R. Scherer et al., “Emotional Experience in Cultural Context: A Comparison Between Europe, Japan and the United States,” in *Facets of Emotion: Recent Research* (Hillsdale, NJ: Erlbaum, 1988), 5–30.

29. P. J. Fite et al., “Reactive and Proactive Aggression in Adolescent Males: Examining Differential Outcomes 10 Years Later in Early Adulthood,” *Criminal Justice and Behavior* 37, no. 2 (2010): 141–57, https://doi: 0.1177/0093854809353051; P. J. Fite et al., *Reactive/Proactive Aggression and the Deveopment of Internalizing Problems in Males: The Moderating Effect of Parent and Peer Relationships, Aggressive Behavior* 40 (2014): 69–78, https://doi:10.1002/ab.21498.

30. H. Hatch and D. K. Forgays, “A Comparison of Older Adolescent and Adult Females’ Responses to Anger-Provoking Situations,” *Adolescence* 36, no. 143 (2001): 557–70.

31. P. J. Fite et al., “Reactive/Proactive Aggression and the Deveopment of Internalizing Problems in Males.”

32. Crick and Dodge, “Social Information-Processing Mechanisms in Reactive and Proactive Aggression”; Dodge, Godwin, and the Conduct Problems Prevention Research Group, “Social-Information-Processing Patterns Mediate the Impact of Preventive Interventio on Adolescent Antisocial Behavior.”

33. Daniel Goleman, *Emotional Intelligence: Why It Can Matter More than IQ* (New York: Bantam Books, 1995).

Resources

Books about Anger for Pre-School & School-Aged Children

1) *Angry Octopus: Learn How to Control Anger, Reduce Stress and Fall Asleep Faster* by Lori Lite
2) *Hands Are Not For Hitting* by Martine Agassi
3) *How to Take the Grrrr Out of Anger* by Elizabeth Verdick and Marjorie Lisovskis
4) *I Am So Angry I Could Scream: Helping Children Deal with Anger* by Laura Fox and and Chris Sabatino
5) *I Hate Everything! A Book About Feeling Angry* by Sue Graves
6) *I'm Not Bad, I'm Just Mad: A Workbook to Help Kids Control Their Anger* by Lawrence Sharpiro, Zack Pelta Heller and Anna Greenwald
7) *I Was So Mad* by Mercer Mayer
8) *Mad Isn't Bad: A Child's Book about Anger* by Mundy Michaelene and R. W. Alley
9) *Pig Wisdom: Anger Management* by B. J. Taylor
10) *¿Puede Pedro el Puercoespín Controlar su Mal Genio? (Zac y sus Amigos)* by Misty Black
11) *Spinky Sulks* by William Steig
12) *Tiger has a Tantrum: A Book about Feeling Angry* by Sue Graves
13) *Train Your Angry Dragon: A Cute Children Story To Teach Kids About Emotions and Anger Management* by Steve Herman
14) *What to Do When Your Temper Flares* by Dawn Huebner
15) *When I Feel Angry* by Corneila Maude Spelman and Nancy Cote
16) *When Sophie Gets Angry – Really, Really Angry* by Molly Bang
17) *Words Are Not for Hurting* by Elizabeth Verdick

Books about Anger for Pre-Adolescent & Adolescents

1) *Coping Skills for Teens Workbook: 60 Helpful Ways to Deal with Stress, Anxiety and Anger* by Janine Halloran
2) *Hot Stuff to Help Kids Chill Out Anger Management Book* by Jerry Wilde
3) *Hot Stuff to Help Kids Chill Out Anger and Stress Management Book* by Jerry Wilde
4) *The Anger Workbook for Teens, Second Edition* by Raychelle Lohmann
5) *The Anxiety, Depression & Anger Toolbox for Teens: 150 Powerful Mindfulness, CBT & Positive Psychology Activities to Manage Emotions* by Jeffrey Bernstein
6) *Zero to 60: A Teen's Guide to Manage Frustration, Anger, and Everyday Irritations* by Michael A. Tompkins

Books and Resources about Anger for Parents

1) *Angry Children, Worried Parents: Seven Steps to Help Families Manage Anger* by Sam Goldstein, Robert Brooks and Sharon Weiss
2) *Anger Management for Parents* by Emma Perez
3) *Anger Management for Parents: How to Manage Your Emotions & Raise a Happy and Confident Child* by Susan Garcia
4) *Anger Management for Parents: Step By Step Guide That Helps You Stop Being Angry As a Parent and Start Learning to Empathize With Your Child* by Elaine A. Hendrickson
5) *Healthy Anger: How to Help Children and Teens Manage Their Anger* by Bernard Golden
6) *How to Stop Losing Your Sh*t with Your Kids: A Practical Guide to Becoming a Calmer, Happier Parent* by Carla Naumburg
7) *Little Volcanoes: Helping Young Children and Their Parents Deal with Anger* by Warwick Pudney
8) *Parenting Toolbox: 125 Activities Therapists Use to Reduce Meltdowns, Increase Positive Behaviors & Manage Emotions* by Lisa Phifer, Laura Sibbald, and Jennifer Roden
9) *Show Me Your Mad Face: Teaching Children to Be Angry Without Losing Control* by Connie Schnoes
10) *The Explosive Child: A New Approach for Understanding and Parenting Easily Frustrated, Chronically Inflexible Children,* Sixth Edition by Ross Greene

11) *The Whole-Brain Child: 12 Revolutionary Strategies to Nurture Your Child's Developing Mind* by Daniel Siegel

Getting Professional Help:

Psychology Today Therapist Directory by location:
https://www.psychologytoday.com/us/therapists/

Books and Resources about Anger for Educators

1) *A Little SPOT of Feelings and Emotions Educator's Guide* by Diane Alber
2) *Anger Management Workbook for Kids: 50 Fun Activities to Help Children Stay Calm and Make Better Choices When They Feel Mad (Health and Wellness Workbooks for Kids)* by Samantha Snowden
3) *Anger Management Skills Workbook for Kids: 40 Awesome Activities to Help Children Calm Down, Cope, and Regain Control* by Amanda Robinson
4) *A Volcanoe in My Tummy* by Elaine Whitehouse and Warwick Pudney
5) *Coping with Conflict: An Elementary Approach* by Diane Senn and Gwen Sitsch
6) *Managing Anger: Lesson Plans. Public Broadcasting System http://www.pbs.org/inthemix/educators/lessons/schoolviol3/*
7) *Seeing Red: An Anger Management and Peacemaking Curriculum for Kids* by Jennifer Simmonds
8) *Take Charge – An Anger Management through Social Problem Solving Curriculum for 6-8th grade, University of Florida, https://education.ufl.edu/behavior-management-resource-guide/take-charge-anger-management-curriculum/*
9) *Therapist Aid: a lot of free worksheets to use individually, in groups, and during classroom lessons,. https://www.therapistaid.com/*
10) *Transforming Anger to Personal Power: An Anger Management Curriculum for Grades 6-12* by Susan A. Gingras Fitzell
11) *10 Days to a Less Defiant Child: The Breakthrough Program for Overcoming Your Child's Difficult Behavior*, Second Edition by Jeffrey Bernstein

About the Author

RAYCHELLE CASSADA LOHMANN, PH.D., LCMHCS, ACS, GCDF is a counselor educator, clinical mental health counselor, and author. She has expertise in a wide range of issues affecting adolescents, from anger and aggression to anxiety and depression to sexual trauma and bullying. Raychelle attended North Carolina State University, where she received her B.A. in psychology, her M.S. in counselor education and her Ph.D. in counseling and counselor education. With over 20 years in the counseling profession, Raychelle has devoted much of her time to working with children, adolescents, parents, and educators. She is passionate about what she does and strives to live out her personal mission statement of "helping others transform their lives from the inside out."